JUST ONE POT

Lindsey Bareham

CONTENTS

Have you ever totted up how much time and energy you waste washing up the sinkful of pans which seem to be required for every meal? Well, neither had I until my cooking life was turned upside down for three months while I had my kitchen ripped out and replaced. Cooking on two burners and using a maximum of two pans for each meal had such a useful effect on my cooking and eliminated so much tedious washing up that I decided to turn the recipes into a book. After all, it seemed to me, if a book will help you provide interesting food for yourself, your family, and your friends without a load of the worst kind of washing up, who could resist it? All the recipes here can be cooked in one, occasionally two, pans (and the second is usually just for preparing vegetables). Some dishes, such as the stews and curries, could be cooked in the oven, but an oven is not essential for any recipe. Occasionally dishes are finished under the broiler, but it's rare and never essential to the goodness of the dish.

Most recipes are simple, requiring minimal preparation, and all are made with easily attainable, seasonal ingredients. There are no fiddly, restaurant-style dishes, but there are plenty of tricks of the trade that will upgrade your daily meals. This is after-work food, the daily meal that shouldn't be too demanding to make or take too long to cook. Equally, these dishes are never boring: there are big soups, piled with fresh, seasonal vegetables, sometimes with fish or meat, which are interesting and satisfying enough to be a complete meal. There are numerous ways of turning the staples of life, such as pasta, potatoes, rice, and dried beans, into meals to remember. Chicken, which is what most of us turn to repeatedly for quick, after-work meals, makes up one of the biggest chapters, including dishes as diverse as Scottish Cock-a-leekie, Thai Chicken tom yam, and French After-work coq au vin. Seafood, which is often overlooked as a healthy, fast food, is another big section, with favorites from all around the world, including Spanish Cod with white beans, After-work bouillabaisse, and Shrimp laksa with green beans. Pork, bacon, and ham is possibly my favorite section, with hearty dishes such as Cocktail sausage and lentil stew and Dublin coddle. Red meats—Lamb and Beef, veal and venison—are the smallest chapters because, like so many people, I eat less red meat than I used to and I'm fussy about its heritage. That's not to say I could ever resist a properly made Irish stew, or less familiar meaty dishes such as Greek lemon lamb with new potatoes, Frito mallorquin (who would have thought liver could taste so good?), and Smoked chili con carne with cherry tomatoes. The Vegetarian section grew so large that I considered devoting the whole book to one-pan vegetarian dishes; the possibilities, it seems to me, are endless. Malaysian Gado gado and Macaroni cheese with melting tomatoes is the kind of food I'm talking about. Desserts, too, get a major look in. Chocolate rice pudding, Scottish Cranachan, Eton mess, and Apple cream with banana passion fruit sauce is my kind of dessert in a bowl.

A word or two about ingredients: **stock** is key to many of these one-pot dishes. While homemade is always desirable, store-bought stock is fine for convenience—quick-dissolving granules, cubes, or even a can of consommé will all do the trick. I peel stringy **vegetables** like celery with a potato peeler, but potatoes I usually cook first, as the skins are then so much easier to remove. When making a **garlic** paste, check cloves for the little green growing stem, and remove it first—but don't bother if you are chopping or slicing it. Always choose unwaxed **lemons** if the zest is to be used in a recipe.

My time of self-inflicted kitchen denial also proved that you need very little equipment to cook well with comfort and efficiency. I limited myself to a couple of sharp knives and a knife sharpener to keep them perfect; a cutting board; a few wooden spoons; a whisk; a skillet and a wok; a large heavy-bottom pan and a small one for milk and eggs; a kettle; and a toaster. I also relied on a good, swivel-head potato peeler, a colander and a strainer, and my trusty food processor.

The book reflects the pleasure I found in the challenge of cooking on two burners, but translates perfectly to all of us, all the time. These dishes prove, simply and tastefully, that cooking in one pan makes a lot of sense.

Lindsey Bareham

Vegetarian

It's interesting how the meat-and-two-veg-loving majority has had a change of heart when it comes to vegetarianism. Less than twenty years ago, if you didn't eat meat you were a bit of a weirdo. Yet look at any fashionable menu now, peppered as it is with dish after dish without meat or fish, or check out the chill counter of any supermarket, and you'll find the choice on offer is extraordinarily diverse. Vegetarian cooking has become a favorite with adventurous cooks, and meals can be a feast for all the senses—a mixture of colors, flavors, and textures. Although I am never likely to give up meat and fish completely, I'm typical of the new breed of quasi-vegetarians who no longer think that meat is essential in a balanced diet. My cooking has changed over recent years toward vegetarianism, prompted as much by food scares as the high price of properly reared meat. Without making a conscious effort, I eat meat-and-fish-free meals at least three times a week, sometimes more often.

Even so, it was quite a shock when I annotated my recipes for inclusion in this book to discover that this section was the largest and most difficult to prune down. Onion and rosemary risotto with Marsala, Autumn vegetable ragout, and Italian arugula and potato soup is the sort of food I'm talking about, as is Potato salad with watercress. These dishes are delicious in their own right, and are satisfying enough, in terms of texture and color as well as flavor, that no one notices the lack of meat. It is the sort of food that keeps us in touch with the seasons. Vegetables are also comparatively simple and inexpensive to shop for; in many places now it is increasingly easy to buy organic vegetables from farmers' markets, regional suppliers, and the supermarkets.

I've found that the more I turn toward a vegetarian diet, the more conscious I am of the effect that certain foods have on my metabolism and general well-being. Information on how food affects us, in terms of mood as well as nutrition, is widely available from many sources and is both interesting and useful to know. Lentils, for example, man's oldest food, are good for reducing cholesterol, stress, and nervous exhaustion, while nature's other comfort food and one of my favorites, the wonderfully versatile potato, is packed with minerals and vitamins.

Asparagus risotto

Serves 4   *10 minutes preparation: 30 minutes cooking*

The useful thing about this risotto is that it doesn't rely on being made with a special stock. Instead, the asparagus cooking liquid is bolstered with stock granules. The cooked stems, as opposed to the tips, are chopped and liquidized with a little of the asparagus stock, and this bright green sauce is stirred into the risotto along with the tender tips, at the end of cooking. The risotto is finished with what seems like a huge amount of grated Parmesan and a knob of butter.

1lb/500g asparagus
½ stick butter
squeeze lemon
1 heaped tsp vegetable stock granules
1 small onion or shallot

scant 1 cup risotto rice
½ wine glass Noilly Prat, vermouth, or white wine
4 heaped tbsp freshly grated Parmesan cheese
   plus extra to serve
salt and freshly ground pepper

Trim and discard the woody ends of the asparagus. Cut off the tender tips and set aside. Cut the remaining stems into chunks. In a suitable pan, bring 3½ cups water to a boil. Add a generous pinch of salt and the asparagus tips. Bring the water back to a boil and cook for 2 minutes. Scoop the tips out of the water and drain. Drop the stems into the water and cook for 4 minutes, or until completely tender. Reduce the heat and scoop out of the pan.

Place the stems and a cup of the cooking water into the bowl of a food processor with a knob of butter. Blitz to make a smooth purée. If necessary, pass the purée through a strainer. Taste and adjust the flavor with salt, pepper, and a squeeze of lemon. Dissolve the stock granules in the rest of the cooking water, then pour into a pitcher or bowl and cover to keep hot.

Peel and finely chop the onion. Melt half the remaining butter in a heavy pan and gently cook the onion until soft but not colored—about 3 minutes. Add the rice and cook with the onion until the rice is glistening and semitranslucent—about 2 minutes. As soon as the rice turns shiny and even more translucent, add the Noilly Prat. It will seethe and then bubble away into the rice, but make sure you stir as it does so. Add a ladleful of the hot stock. Stir as it sizzles and then cook for a couple of minutes, stirring constantly, until the rice has absorbed most of the liquid. Add a second ladleful of stock and stir until all the liquid is absorbed, adjusting the heat to maintain a gentle simmer.

Continue in this way, stirring constantly, until the rice is almost tender but firm to the bite, about 20–30 minutes in total. The risotto should have a creamy, porridge-like consistency. Remove from the heat. Stir in the asparagus purée, the asparagus tips, the remaining butter, and the cheese. Cover and let stand for 5 minutes to finish cooking. Serve sprinkled with extra Parmesan.

Cherry tomato gazpacho

Serves 6–8   *25 minutes preparation*

The great thing about using cherry tomatoes for Spanish gazpacho, as opposed to regular tomatoes, is that their flavor is reliably intense. Gazpacho is the perfect thing to eat on a hot day. It's often described as the salad soup because it's made with ingredients that would make a fine salad. When served with its full complement of garnishes, as here, it becomes a meal in itself.

4 thick slices white bread, without crusts, about
   5oz/150g
2 plump garlic cloves, peeled
1 cucumber
1 red chile
2 red bell peppers (the extra-"sweet" pointed type)
1 red onion
2lb/1kg cherry tomatoes or ripe vine tomatoes

2 tbsp sherry vinegar or wine vinegar
1¼ cups cold water
about 20 mint leaves
scant ½ cup olive oil plus 2 tbsp
3 plum or vine tomatoes
squeeze lemon juice
Tabasco sauce
salt and freshly ground black pepper

Tear the bread into pieces. Place it and the peeled garlic in the bowl of a food processor and blitz to make fine bread crumbs.

Peel the cucumber. Halve it lengthwise and use a teaspoon to scrape out the seeds. Chop half coarsely. Trim and split the chile and scrape out the seeds. Set aside half of one red bell pepper and chop the rest, discarding seeds and white membrane. Peel and halve the onion. Coarsely chop one half and add to the bread crumbs in the food processor bowl together with the chopped cucumber, chile, and chopped red bell pepper.

Remove the stems from the cherry tomatoes and add them to the food processor bowl with the vinegar, water, most of the mint, the scant ½ cup olive oil, ½ teaspoon of salt, and a generous seasoning of black pepper. Blitz for several minutes until liquidized.

Meanwhile, prepare the garnishes. Keeping separate piles, finely dice the remaining cucumber and red bell pepper and finely chop the remaining red onion. Cut the plum tomatoes into fourths, then discard the seeds and chop finely. Taste the gazpacho and adjust the seasoning with salt, pepper, lemon juice, and Tabasco. Transfer to a chilled serving bowl and decorate with a swirl of olive oil. Serve with the garnishes in small bowls, adding the remaining mint leaves to the tomato.

Autumn vegetable ragout

Serves 4–6 *20 minutes preparation: 30 minutes cooking*

Cold, damp weather is comfort-food time. A steaming bowl of chunky vegetables is the culinary equivalent of a nice warm hug. I hesitate to call this a big bowlful soup because the proportion of vegetables to liquid makes it more like a stew. The trick here is to cook the vegetables in the right order for the right length of time so that the background stuff, like potatoes and onions, is soft and tender and the green vegetables keep a bit of bite. Chile and garlic are added at the beginning to lend soul rather than fire. If you feel inclined, cover each bowl with grated Cheddar or Parmesan and add a dollop of pesto. I like to dip big slabs of garlic-rubbed toast into the soup.

1 onion	1 leek
2 large garlic cloves	1 vegetable stock cube dissolved in 4 cups
1 red chile	boiling water
3 tbsp olive oil	1lb/450g broccoli florets
4 potatoes	handful of snow peas or sugar snap peas
1 large carrot	salt and freshly ground black pepper
1 red bell pepper	lemon wedges to serve

Peel and halve the onion and garlic, then finely chop. Trim and split the chile, then wipe away the seeds and finely chop. Don't forget to wash your hands now with soapy water to get rid of the lethal chile juices that will burn sensitive parts.

Gently soften the onion, garlic, and chile in the olive oil in a decent-size, heavy-bottom pan placed over medium-low heat. Stir every so often while you get chopping. Peel the potatoes, then chop into kabob-size chunks and rinse. Peel the carrots and chop slightly smaller. Stir the potatoes and carrots into the softened and lightly browned onions and season generously with salt and black pepper. Cover and cook, stirring once or twice, for 5 minutes.

Meanwhile, finely chop the red bell pepper, discarding seeds and white membrane, and thickly slice the white part of the leek; keep the greens for later. Stir the red bell pepper and leek white into the pan, then cover again and let stand for a few more minutes before adding the stock. Return the pan to a boil, then reduce the heat slightly and cook, uncovered, for 5–6 minutes, or until the potatoes are just tender.

Cut the broccoli into bite-size florets and slice down the snow peas to make 3 or 4 strips. Finely slice the leek greens and wash thoroughly. Add all three to the pot, then taste the broth and adjust the seasoning. Boil steadily for 2–3 minutes, or until you are satisfied that the broccoli is *al dente*. Serve immediately with a wedge of lemon to squeeze over the top.

Fattoush

Serves 4–6 *30 minutes preparation: 2 minutes cooking*

Fattoush is a Middle Eastern salad which pops up on many Lebanese menus. To be really authentic, you will need to hunt out a blend of Middle Eastern herbs called za'atar which includes a tart, red spice called sumac. This is the red dust that decorates and seasons much Middle Eastern food, and is often sprinkled over onion salads. I'm not convinced that any of these extra sharp, resinous flavors are essential to the success of the already acidic and nutty salad. To get maximum pleasure from making this salad, you will need two sharp knives: one small triangular paring knife and a larger broad-pointed cook's knife. This is most definitely a salad that is all about chopping and slicing and it will be misery to attempt with a blunt knife.

1 cucumber	2 plump garlic cloves
4 large shallots or 3½oz/100g bunch scallions	juice 1 lemon
or 2 medium red onions	6 tbsp olive oil
1lb/500g tomatoes	1 tbsp coarsely chopped mint
1 celery heart or 4 peeled stalks	3 tbsp coarsely chopped cilantro
1 slice pita bread	salt and freshly ground black pepper
1 large bunch flatleaf parsley, at least 3oz/85g	

Use a potato peeler to peel the cucumber, then split lengthwise and use a teaspoon to gouge out the seeds. Cut into lengths and dice the flesh. Tip into a colander, then dredge with 1 tablespoon salt and let drain while you do all the rest of the chopping.

Peel and finely dice the shallots. Place the tomatoes in a bowl and cover with boiling water, then count to 20 and drain. Cut the tomatoes into fourths and flake away the skin. Use your fingers or a teaspoon to remove the seeds. Dice the flesh. Trim and very finely slice the celery, then tip into a colander and rinse thoroughly under cold running water. Drain carefully.

Split the pita bread in half and toast both sides until crisp. When cool enough to handle, crumble up the bread into small pieces. Pick all the leaves off the parsley stems and chop very finely. Peel the garlic, chop coarsely, then sprinkle with a scant ½ teaspoon of salt and pulverize with the flat of a blade to make a creamy paste. Tip the garlic paste into a salad bowl, then stir in the lemon juice and whisk in the olive oil. Tip in the onions, then the celery, and finally the tomatoes and herbs, stirring as you make each addition.

Rinse the salt from the cucumber, then drain thoroughly and pat dry with paper towels. Add to the salad and season generously with black pepper. Give one final toss and strew the pita bread crumbs over the top. Five minutes before you are ready to eat, fold in the crumbs.

Eggs masala

Serves 4   *15 minutes preparation: 40 minutes cooking*

*If you have a can of tomatoes in the pantry, you are never very far from a delicious supper.
If you also have a couple of onions, some eggs, and a decent collection of Indian spices, you can
knock up this lovely curry supper. There is something immensely pleasing about the texture and
mild flavor of hard-cooked eggs with a thick and chunky tomato and onion curry spiked at the
last moment with a handful of cilantro. It is delicious with warmed Indian bread to scoop and
mop, but becomes more of a meal with rice, poppadoms, and your favorite pickles.*

4 garlic cloves
1in/2.5cm piece fresh gingerroot
2 cardamom pods
1 tsp coriander seeds
1 tsp cumin seeds
½ tsp whole cloves
½ tsp black peppercorns
½ tsp cayenne pepper

1lb/500g ripe tomatoes or 14oz/400g canned
   chopped tomatoes
6–8 eggs, hard-cooked
2 large onions
2 tbsp vegetable oil
lemon juice
2 tbsp cilantro leaves
salt

Peel and chop the garlic. Peel and grate the ginger. Remove the seeds from the 4 cardamom
pods. Grind the cardamom, coriander seeds, cumin, cloves, and black peppercorns to a powder
in a food processor or coffee grinder and then add the garlic, ginger, and 2 tablespoons of
water. Blitz to make a stiff masala paste and stir in the cayenne pepper.

If using ripe tomatoes, pour boiling water over them and count to 20, then drain. Remove the
core and peel, then coarsely chop. Peel the hard-cooked eggs and halve lengthwise.

Meanwhile, peel and finely dice the onions. Heat the oil in a wok or large pan over medium-
high heat and cook the onions until they turn caramel brown, stirring constantly so they brown
evenly. Allow at least 20 minutes. Stir the masala paste into the onions and stir-fry for a
couple of minutes. Add the tomatoes and a generous pinch of salt. Simmer vigorously for
10–15 minutes, or until the sauce begins to thicken. Taste and adjust the seasoning with
more salt and lemon juice. If the tomatoes weren't ripe enough, you may need to add a little
sugar and a slug of ketchup.

Get the sauce very hot, then stir in most of the cilantro and place the eggs, sunny-side up, in
the sauce. Continue simmering until the eggs are warmed through. Sprinkle on the last of the
cilantro and serve with basmati rice, raita, and mango chutney.

Fragrant mushroom curry with green beans

Serves 4   *15 minutes preparation: 35 minutes cooking*

This isn't an overly hot curry, more of a fragrant gravy with a gentle back heat, but a sensible and delicious accompaniment would be a bowl of raita or thick plain yogurt stirred with grated cucumber. I like to serve it with basmati rice or warm naan bread or chapatis to scoop up the copious and delicious juices. If you eat seafood, a good addition to this curry, in terms of flavor, texture, and color, is a handful of cooked shrimp, added just before the garam masala.

1 large onion
2 tbsp cooking oil
1 plump red chile, about 3in x 1½in/7cm x 3cm
generous 1¼ cups green beans
2 rounded tsp curry powder
7fl oz/200ml carton coconut cream
½ chicken stock cube dissolved in 1 cup
   boiling water

1lb/500g white mushrooms or medium mushrooms
   cut into fourths
2 medium tomatoes
squeeze lemon juice
1 rounded tsp garam masala
handful cilantro leaves
salt and freshly ground black pepper

Peel, then halve and finely chop the onion. Add the oil and then the onion to a spacious, heavy-bottom pan placed over medium-low heat. Cook, stirring often, for 10–15 minutes, or until the onion is soft but uncolored. Meanwhile, trim and split the chile and scrape away the seeds. Chop into tiny dice. Stir the chile into the onions and cook for a couple of minutes while you trim the beans (I never remove the pointed ends) and cut them in half.

Stir the curry powder into the onions and cook, stirring constantly, for 2 more minutes. Add the beans to the pan, then increase the heat slightly and cook, stirring every so often, for 3 minutes. Add the coconut cream and the stock, then give the dish a good stir and let simmer for a couple of minutes. Wipe the mushrooms and add them to the pan. Cook, stirring often, for about 8 minutes, or until cooked through.

Chop the tomatoes (I would peel and seed them, but skin and seed don't spoil the dish) and stir them into the curry. Cook for a few more minutes until warmed through. Now taste the gravy and adjust the seasoning with salt, pepper, and lemon juice. Sprinkle over the garam masala and cook for 1 more minute, then serve strewn with cilantro leaves.

Gado gado

Serves 4   *25 minutes preparation: 15 minutes cooking*

Gado gado is excellent refrigerator-tidying food. It's an Indonesian vegetable salad dressed with a spicy peanut sauce, and almost anything goes. What you're aiming at is a good mixture of crisp, crunchy textures, so make sure you include bean sprouts, green beans, cucumber, and carrot. Hard-cooked egg is always present and the warm salad is often turned into more of a meal by the addition of fried tofu. The satay-style, spicy peanut sauce saves the salad from blandness. In restaurants, gado gado is arranged in layers on a large platter as part of a spread. When serving it as family fare, it is wiser to make four separate plates.

10oz/300g block tofu/beancurd
1 large carrot
½ small white cabbage
scant 1 cup green beans
scant 1¼ cups young spinach leaves
2 Boston lettuce hearts
1 small cucumber
2 potatoes, boiled and peeled
4 shallots or 2 small red onions

7oz/200g cauliflower or broccoli florets
⅔ cup bean sprouts
3 tbsp vegetable oil
2 tbsp flour
2 eggs, hard-cooked
4 tbsp satay peanut sauce or 3 tbsp peanut butter thinned with lime or lemon juice, water, and Tabasco
salt

Place the tofu on a plate and weight with a second plate to draw out the liquid. Meanwhile, put a large pan of water on to boil. Keeping separate piles, prepare the vegetables. Peel the carrot and slice into short, thin sticks. Halve the cabbage and cut out the core, then slice thinly across the wedge. Trim the green beans and cut in half. Shred the spinach. Finely shred the lettuce, then wash and dry. Peel the cucumber and slice finely. Chop the potatoes. Peel, then halve and finely slice the shallots.

Generously salt the boiling water. Add the carrots, then bring back to a boil and boil for 1 minute. Scoop into a colander. Repeat with the cabbage, beans, and cauliflower. Transfer the drained vegetables to a large mixing bowl. Now place the bean sprouts in the colander, then pour over the cooking water and shake to drain. Add bean sprouts, spinach, lettuce, and cucumber to the bowl and lightly toss everything together.

Arrange the salad in a pyramid on four dinner plates. Scatter the chopped potatoes on top. Heat the oil in the pan while you pat dry the tofu and cut it into strips. Toss the strips in the flour and cook quickly in hot oil until lightly golden. Remove from the pan to drain and add the shallots to the pan. Cook quickly until crisp and golden. Drain. Add the tofu to the salad and decorate with wedges of hard-cooked egg, then pour over the peanut sauce and sprinkle with the fried shallots.

Goanese potato curry

Serves 2–4   *30 minutes preparation: 30 minutes cooking*

This wonderful potato curry is rich and interesting enough to serve on its own. It is good, too, with hard-cooked eggs cut into fourths and a handful of boiled green beans stirred into the curry at the last moment. I like it scooped up in hot Indian bread with raita and mango chutney. If you need a serious carbohydrate fix, and I admit this is one of my favorite night-after-the-night-before meals, serve it with rice and dal. Coconut cream, incidentally, is pressed and processed fresh coconut and is sold in convenient 7fl oz/200ml cartons. I always keep one or two in the pantry because I prefer its thick creaminess to canned coconut. Or you can use canned or creamed coconut—the one that looks like a slab of shortening—made up to package directions.

1lb 10oz/750g new potatoes	7fl oz/200ml carton coconut cream
2 onions	1lb/500g tomatoes
2 tbsp vegetable oil	1 cup frozen baby peas
1 small red or green chile	1 lime
3 garlic cloves	handful cilantro leaves
3 tsp ground cinnamon	salt and freshly ground black pepper
2 tsp coriander seeds or 3 tsp ground coriander	

Peel and rinse the potatoes, then boil them in plenty of salted water until tender to the point of a knife. Drain and let cool. Meanwhile, peel and halve the onions, then thinly slice. Heat the oil in a spacious skillet or similarly wide-based pan until very hot. Stir in the onions and let them brown lightly. Reduce the heat and cook, stirring occasionally, for about 10 minutes, or until limp and soft.

Meanwhile, trim and split the chile and scrape away the seeds. Chop. Peel and chop the garlic. Stir the chile, garlic, cinnamon, and coriander seeds into the onions and cook for a couple of minutes before adding the coconut cream. Simmer gently for 5 minutes, then remove and liquidize the mixture to make a thick, creamy, speckled beige sauce. Return the sauce to the skillet.

Pour boiling water over the tomatoes and count to 20, then drain and peel. Chop the tomatoes and place in a pan with 1 cup water. Boil for about 10 minutes, then strain the tomatoes directly into the sauce, pressing hard to extract maximum pulp. Cut the potatoes into bite-size chunks and add them too. Finally, cook the baby peas in boiling salted water and add them to the dish. Season generously with salt and lightly with pepper. Cook for a few minutes, then squeeze over the lime juice. Taste and adjust the seasoning. Garnish with cilantro leaves and serve. Excellent hot, warm, or cold.

Italian arugula and potato soup

Serves 2 *15 minutes preparation: 30 minutes cooking*

It's hard to believe that such an ordinary collection of ingredients makes such a delicious soup. I came across zuppa dei poveri con la rucola *years ago when I was doing research for a book. It's been a regular treat ever since and I make it whenever I have a few leftover boiled potatoes in need of using up. It's known as poor man's soup because potatoes, bread, and arugula, which grows like a weed in Italy and anywhere it gets a chance to establish itself, are regarded as peasant food. My version ends up thick and rustic and the flavors are enriched with stock, garlic, and olive oil. A sprig of rosemary scents the soup with its wild woodland flavors and the last-minute garnish of a splash of extra virgin olive oil enriches and unifies all the ingredients.*

9oz/250g salad or other waxy potatoes
1 vegetable stock cube
1 onion
1 plump garlic clove
1 tbsp olive oil

1 sprig rosemary
2oz/55g stale or unbaked ciabatta bread
3½ oz/100g arugula
3 tbsp extra virgin olive oil
salt and freshly ground black pepper

Boil the unpeeled potatoes in plenty of salted water until tender. Drain, measuring off scant 3 cups of the cooking water, then return the potatoes to the pan and cover with cold water. Let stand for a couple of minutes, then drain again and remove the skins. Cut into chunks.

Dissolve the stock cube in the reserved potato water. Meanwhile, peel and halve the onion and garlic, then chop. Heat the tablespoon of oil in a heavy-bottom pan and stir in the onion, garlic, and rosemary. Cook, stirring often, for about 8 minutes, or until the onions are soft but not crisp. Meanwhile, chop the bread into bite-sized chunks.

Stir in the potatoes and add the stock, then season with salt and pepper and bring the liquid to a boil. Stir in the arugula, then reduce the heat and, as soon as it is wilted, add the bread, stirring it as it drinks up the soup and softens. Dribble over the extra virgin olive oil and remove from the heat, then cover and let stand for a few minutes before serving with a final twist of pepper.

Greek potato salad with cilantro

Serves 4   *15 minutes preparation: 15 minutes cooking*

I could never give up potatoes for very long. I love them so much that I wrote a book, In Praise of the Potato, *devoted to them. I chose this recipe from the chapter on potato salads and it goes with everything from a slab of feta and a hard-cooked egg, to fish, chicken, or lamb. This latest version ups the quantity of cilantro and specifies red rather than any other onion. The result is a very pretty salad streaked with red and thick with green leaves. It is the perfect thing for a barbecue when you might echo the Greek theme with hummus, taramasalata, stuffed grape leaves, a Greek salad, and lamb kabobs. Stuff the lot into warmed split Greek bread. Yum.*

1lb 10oz/750g similar-size new potatoes
1 red onion
2 garlic cloves
2½oz/65g bunch cilantro

2 tbsp wine vinegar
4 tbsp good quality extra virgin olive oil
salt and freshly ground black pepper

Scrub or peel the potatoes and rinse, then cook in plenty of salted boiling water until tender. Drain. Leave small potatoes whole, halve medium potatoes, and cut large ones into chunks.

Meanwhile, peel and halve the onion, then finely slice. Peel and chop the garlic. Trim the coarse stem ends of the bunch of cilantro. Keeping the bunch shape, finely chop the stems and let the chopping get progressively coarser as you work up the bunch into the leaves.

Pour the vinegar into a salad bowl and add a generous pinch of salt and several grinds of black pepper. Swirl the vinegar around the bowl until the salt has dissolved. Whisk in the olive oil to make a thick and luscious dressing. Stir in the garlic and onion and then add the hot potatoes. Stir thoroughly and add the chopped cilantro. Stir again and serve hot, warm, or cold, giving a final stir just before serving.

Macaroni cheese with melting tomatoes

Serves 4   *15 minutes preparation: 15 minutes cooking*

When I think of macaroni cheese—and Monday night, with its combination of an empty pantry, minimal interest in shopping and cooking, and the need for something comforting to eat—is when it usually happens, I imagine it with a crusty, cheesy topping. This equally delicious version is risotto-style: sloppy and gorgeous. Non-vegetarians may choose to add crunch from crisp nuggets of fried smoked pancetta or bacon, added straight after the macaroni.

4 tomatoes, halved
1 tbsp olive oil
1¾ cups macaroni
3½oz/100g bunch scallions
¼ stick butter
2 tablespoons all-purpose flour

½ tbsp smooth Dijon mustard
1¼ cups milk
5oz/150g hard cheese, grated, plus extra to serve
chives to serve
salt and freshly ground black pepper

First cook the tomatoes. This can be done under the broiler, in the oven, in a skillet, or in the pasta pan before the pasta. If broiling or cooking in the oven, smear the cut surfaces with olive oil; if frying, add the oil to the pan and cook gently until completely soft. Allow at least 10 minutes for this. Next, cook the macaroni in plenty of salted boiling water according to the package directions. Drain and cover to keep warm.

Meanwhile, trim and finely slice the scallions. Add the butter to the pan, then stir in the onions and cook for a couple of minutes until softened. Stir in the flour, continuing until it disappears. Add the mustard and gradually incorporate the milk, beating briskly as it begins to boil to make a smooth sauce. Reduce the heat and cook gently for about 5 minutes to cook the flour. Stir in the cheese. Taste and adjust the seasoning with salt and pepper.

Stir the macaroni into the sauce. Serve risotto-style with a garnish of grated cheese and chopped chives and the tomatoes on the side.

Moroccan salad

Serves 2   *15 minutes preparation: 15 minutes cooking*

I once stayed at the most amazing "hotel" just outside Marrakech where guests came together in a candlelit garden restaurant. The meal began with the ubiquitous Moroccan salad, a dish that features all over Morocco and is never the same twice, even at the same restaurant. This time it was served mezze-style in a series of dishes. Green lentils came with slivers of red onion; grated carrot and zucchini were seasoned with cilantro and cumin; and crescents of cucumber had been pickled and sweetened with sugar and served icy cold. Another dish contained peeled and semi-carved radishes, another a sweet tomato jelly that was so thick it could be carved into ridges. This stupendous feast was served with a wheel of flat bread decorated with different seeds, and was virtually a meal in itself. My ersatz version makes a satisfying, healthy supper with toasted pita or another flat bread such as focaccia and crisp lettuce leaves to scoop it up.

12 small scrubbed new potatoes

4 tomatoes

1 tsp ground cumin

1 tsp runny honey

4 tbsp olive oil

1 cup green beans

1 carrot

1 small red onion

14oz/400g canned green lentils

1 small lemon

2 tbsp chopped cilantro

salt and freshly ground black pepper

Cook the potatoes in salted boiling water until tender. Drain and let cool. Halve the tomatoes, slicing round tomatoes through their plump middles and plum tomatoes lengthwise. Season each half with a pinch of cumin, salt, and pepper. Dribble with a little honey and olive oil. Pre-heat the broiler to medium. Arrange the tomato halves on the broiler pan and cook, checking so they don't burn, for about 10 minutes, or until very soft.

Meanwhile, put a pan of water on for the beans. Trim the beans (I don't bother to remove the pointy ends) and cut in half. Cook the beans in boiling water for 2 minutes. Drain. Trim and peel the carrot. Grate it through a small hole on the cheese grater or appropriate attachment of a food processor.

Peel and halve the onion and slice wafer-thin. Tip the lentils into a strainer and rinse under cold water. Shake dry. Squeeze the lemon juice into a salad bowl. Add the rest of the cumin and a pinch of salt and pepper and whisk in the remaining olive oil. Stir in the onion, then add the potatoes, beans, carrot, lentils, and cilantro. Toss well and arrange the tomatoes over the top.

Onion and rosemary risotto with Marsala

Serves 2 *15 minutes preparation: 30 minutes cooking*

This is a terrific pantry risotto to warm up a chilly fall night. It demands few fresh ingredients, but the combination of onion, rosemary, and Marsala creates a deliciously rich flavor. The rice should be soft and creamy on the outside with a slight bite on the inside. If it isn't, just add a little more hot water and continue simmering for a few more minutes.

2 medium-size onions and 1 small onion
1 heaped tsp of rosemary leaves
1 tbsp vegetable oil
¾ stick butter
scant 1¼ cups risotto rice
1 small glass Marsala

approximately 4 cups hot vegetable stock
  (fresh is best, but cube is fine)
½ cup grated Parmesan cheese, plus extra
  to serve
pinch sugar
salt and freshly ground black pepper

Peel and halve all 3 onions, then thinly slice, keeping the small slices in a pile on their own. Very finely chop the rosemary leaves to resemble green dust. Cook the small onion in hot vegetable oil in a medium-size heavy-bottom pan (large enough to hold the entire dish), tossing it around until crisp. Drain on absorbent paper towels. Melt ½ stick of the butter in the pan over medium heat. Stir in the large sliced onions and season with ½ teaspoon salt, then cover the pan and cook for about 15 minutes, or until limp.

Stir the rosemary into the limp onions. Add the rice and cook with the onion for a couple of minutes, or until the rice is glistening and semitranslucent. As soon as the rice turns shiny and even more translucent, add the Marsala. It will seethe, then bubble away into the rice, but make sure you stir as it does so. Add a ladleful of hot stock. Stir as it sizzles, stirring constantly and cooking for a couple of minutes, or until the rice has absorbed most of the liquid. Add a second ladleful of stock and stir until all the liquid is absorbed, adjusting the heat to maintain a gentle simmer. Continue in this way, stirring constantly, until the rice is almost tender but firm to the bite—between 20 and 30 minutes in total, or until the risotto has a creamy, porridge-like consistency.

Remove the pan from the heat. Stir in the remaining butter and the cheese. Cover the pan and let stand for 5 minutes before adjusting the seasoning with salt, pepper, and a little sugar. Serve with a garnish of the crisply fried onions and extra Parmesan.

One-eye bouillabaisse with peas

Serves 2 *20 minutes preparation: 15 minutes cooking*

Most people know bouillabaisse, the Mediterranean fishermen's soup. The one-eye version—made with vegetables and eggs—is far less exacting than the original, but is nonetheless a wonderful dish and something to make in the summer when fresh peas and slim leeks are available. This bouillabaisse is more rustic than the famous fish soup, but the principles are identical. Bouillabiasse is named after a method of cooking—bouillon-abaisse—meaning broth rapidly boiled to reduce. More olive oil than you would have thought necessary goes into it, but part of the point of the boiling process is to homogenize the oil with the cooking water. This results in a rich and surprisingly tasty broth also flavored by garlic, orange zest, a bay leaf and a few sprigs of thyme, and rosemary too. A generous pinch of saffron stamens is the only luxury ingredient, and in this bouillabaisse it haunts rather than dominates the flavoring, as is often the case in the fish versions dished up in the Mediterranean.

1 leek	1 bay leaf
1 shallot or small red onion	2 strips paper-thin orange zest
3 large garlic cloves	pinch saffron stamens, dissolved in 1 tbsp
2 large tomatoes	boiling water
1 small zucchini	1¾ cups peas (shelled) or frozen baby peas
6 new potatoes	2 eggs
5 tbsp olive oil	2 thick slices country-style bread
3 sprigs thyme	1 tbsp finely chopped flatleaf parsley
1 small sprig rosemary	salt and freshly ground black pepper

Trim the leek and slice into ½in/1cm circles; rinse and drain. Peel the shallot and chop. Peel the garlic, then slice two of the cloves thinly and cut the third in half. Cover the tomatoes with boiling water. Count to 20, then drain, core, and peel. Remove the seeds and chop the flesh.

Chop the zucchini into small pieces, discarding the ends. Peel the potatoes and slice into thick disks, then rinse and shake dry. Place 4 tablespoons of the olive oil into a large pan over medium heat and briefly cook the leek and shallot with the sliced garlic, thyme, rosemary, bay leaf, and orange zest. Add the saffron, 2½ cups boiling water, the potatoes, and the tomatoes, and season generously with salt and pepper. Increase the heat to the highest possible setting and boil for 5–6 minutes, or until the potatoes are tender. Add the peas and zucchini and cook until tender. Taste and adjust the seasoning.

When the soup is ready, reduce the heat and crack the eggs into it. Simmer gently until the eggs are set. Meanwhile, toast the bread and rub with the cut garlic. Place the toast in two soup bowls and dribble with the remaining olive oil. Using a slotted spoon, lift the egg onto the toast and spoon vegetables around it. Pour on the broth. Sprinkle with parsley and eat.

Potato salad with watercress

Serves 2–4   *20 minutes preparation: 15 minutes cooking*

You can't go wrong with potato salad. Not, that is, if you make it yourself and use decent ingredients for the dressing. This one was inspired by a recipe of French chef Joel Robuchon. My version of this great chef's watercress potato salad is more homespun than the original, but is none the worse for that. Two of us shared the salad and nothing but a smear of dressing was left in the bowl, although M. Robuchon suggests that the dish will feed four to six people. It went down very nicely with slices of prosciutto, farmhouse Cheddar, and crusty bread and butter.

1lb/500g new potatoes (a waxy or salad
  variety such as Charlotte)
2 eggs, hard-cooked
1 shallot
2 scant tbsp white wine vinegar
6 scant tbsp olive oil

3 tbsp finely chopped flatleaf parsley
2 tbsp finely sliced chives
1 tbsp finely chopped mint
2oz/55g trimmed and washed watercress
salt and freshly ground black pepper

Scrape new potatoes with flaky skins, but leave smooth-skinned varieties with skins intact. Boil in plenty of salted water until tender to the point of a knife. Drain. Return smooth-skinned varieties to cold water and let stand for 1 minute before removing the skins. Peel the eggs, preferably while still hot.

While the potatoes cook, peel and halve, then finely chop the shallot. Place the vinegar in a salad bowl and season with salt and pepper. When the salt has dissolved, whisk in the oil to make a thick emulsion. Stir the shallot into the vinaigrette. Slice the hot potatoes directly into the dressing and stir well. Let stand for a few minutes for the dressing to soak into and flavor the potatoes, then grate the eggs directly over the top. The dish looks prettiest if you force the eggs through a small hole on the grater, but you will have to scratch out the clogged holes.

Season with black pepper and a little salt and pile on the chopped herbs. Gently stir everything together. Now pile the watercress on top. Serve immediately while the potatoes are still warm but not hot enough to wilt the watercress.

Salsa cruda tortilla pizza

Serves 2–4   *10 minutes preparation: 5 minutes cooking*

Soft flour tortillas, the sort used in numerous ways in countless Mexican dishes and more recently as sandwich wraps, make a brilliant standby for quick, interesting suppers. Given a quick blast of heat to make them puff and crisp, they make surprisingly good, lightweight pizza bases for almost any food, and don't require cooking. Try white mushrooms fried with garlic and parsley, stirred into a spicy tomato sauce, for example. This "pizza" is spread with pesto, then generously piled with a colorful, chunky salsa-cum-salad which looks as good as it tastes. A generous crumble of feta or goat cheese makes the pizza amazingly satisfying. I'd say you need two each for supper, but one makes a great appetizer.

14oz/400g cherry tomatoes
10 cornichons or 1 small pickled cucumber
15 good-quality black olives
about 15 basil leaves
7oz/200g feta or semihard goat cheese
4 tbsp pesto

1 tbsp lemon juice
1 tbsp olive oil
1 tbsp vegetable oil
4 flour tortillas
sea salt and freshly ground black pepper

To make the salsa cruda, cut the cherry tomatoes into fourths, then scoop the pieces onto a big plate or into a mixing bowl. Cut the cornichons into fourths lengthwise and then slice across into little chunks. Slice the flesh off the olives in 3 or 4 pieces. Add the cornichons and olives to the tomatoes. Season lightly with salt and generously with black pepper.

Shred the basil over the salad and crumble the feta on top. If using a firmer goat cheese, chop it finely. Loosely mix the ingredients. Spoon 1 tablespoon of the pesto into a small bowl and stir in the lemon juice and olive oil. Heat a skillet with a quarter of the vegetable oil or an un-oiled grill pan for a couple of minutes until very hot. If using a grill pan, lightly smear both sides of the tortilla with oil. Lay out a tortilla, pressing it down with a spatula for a few seconds, as it immediately begins to puff and brown underneath. Turn and cook the other side. Repeat to cook the remaining tortilla.

Spread the tortilla with the undiluted pesto, then pile the salsa cruda on top. Give the pesto dressing a final stir and dribble it over the top of the pizzas. Serve immediately.

Spaghetti with garlic, chile, and herbs

Serves 2   *15 minutes preparation: 15 minutes cooking*

This is an incredibly quick, simple, and delicious pasta dish. Apart from the herbs, which are an optional add-on to a classic combination, this is the ultimate pantry fail-safe, midweek supper. Hot pasta is bathed in olive oil flecked with scraps of garlic and chile and masses of chopped herbs: it is hot and fiery but addictive. Adding a hint of mint with the cilantro seems to offset all the flavors while bringing them together. There are so many variations on this simple meal. Try it without the chile and herbs, and if you are a garlic lover, try the garlic raw, letting the heat of the pasta encourage its aroma. It makes a difference, too, if it's made with fresh or dried chile. In the summer it seems more appropriate to make it with fresh chile and in the winter to bump up the heat with dried chile. Ring the changes with different herbs. Flatleaf parsley is always good with garlic. Other herbs that go well in this dish, either alone or in a combination, are basil, mint, and chives. Serve with a glass or two of red wine.

9oz/250g spaghetti
4 garlic cloves
1 red chile or ½ tsp dried chili flakes
1½oz/30g bunch cilantro or flatleaf parsley

few mint leaves
6 tbsp olive oil
salt and freshly ground black pepper

Bring a large pan of water to a boil. Add salt and then the pasta and cook until *al dente* following the package instructions, usually about 12 minutes. Drain, saving about 2 tablespoons of cooking water. Return both the pasta and water to the pan and keep warm.

Meanwhile, peel the garlic and chop finely. Trim the chile and split lengthwise. Scrape away the seeds, then slice into skinny strips and chop into tiny scraps. Discard the bulk of the cilantro stems. Add the mint leaves and chop the herbs together. When the pasta is ready, add the olive oil to a skillet, then warm through and add the garlic. Cook briefly, stirring constantly, for about 30 seconds, and then add the chile. Cook for an additional 30 seconds, or until the garlic is patched very pale brown, but make sure it doesn't darken, or it will turn bitter. Add the contents of the garlic pan to the pasta together with the chopped herbs.

Toss thoroughly until all the pasta is sliding around in its delicious oil. Serve immediately. Do not be tempted to serve this with grated Parmesan or another cheese. There is enough going on without it.

Spanish lentil soup with green olives and pimiento

Serves 2–4   *20 minutes preparation: 40 minutes cooking*

Looking in the pantry for something to liven up the end of a package of French lentils led to this lovely soup. It gets its Spanish connection from those intensely flavored Spanish roast piquillo pimientos (small, pointed red bell peppers), which are now widely available in supermarkets and delicatessens. The other Spanish ingredient is green olives. The soup smells wonderful as it cooks and looks cheerful and inviting with scraps of red bell pepper, lemon zest, green olives, and flatleaf parsley bobbing around in the lentil-thick broth. Each mouthful is a lively contrast of creamy and sharp flavors and, like most lentil-based soups, it's extremely filling.

1 large red onion
3 garlic cloves
1 tbsp olive oil
½ tsp fresh thyme leaves or generous pinch of dried
1 unwaxed lemon
10 large or 20 small green olives
4 roasted piquillo pimiento red peppers, sold in jars

½ cup French lentils
½ tbsp flour
1 vegetable stock cube dissolved in 2½ cups hot water
1 tbsp finely chopped flatleaf parsley
salt and freshly ground black pepper

Peel and halve the onion. Chop half and finely slice the other half. Peel and chop the garlic. Heat the olive oil in a medium-size, heavy-bottom, lidded pan and stir in the onion, garlic, and thyme. Cook briskly, stirring often, for about 8 minutes, or until the onion wilts and begins to brown.

Meanwhile, use a potato peeler to remove the zest from the lemon in wafer-thin, long sheets. Cut into chunky scraps. Give the olives a good bash with something heavy to loosen the pits and then tear or chop into pieces. Cut the peppers in half, then open them out like a book and pile them on top of each other. Chop through the pile to make postage-stamp-size pieces. Stir the lemon zest and then the lentils into the onion and cook, stirring constantly, for a couple of minutes. Now add the olives and peppers. Stir well, then dust the surface with flour and quickly stir it into the lentils until it disappears.

Squeeze half the lemon into the lentils, then add the stock and stir thoroughly while increasing the heat. Bring the soup to a boil. Reduce the heat slightly, then cover the pan and let simmer for 30 minutes. Check the lentils are done, cooking for a few more minutes if they aren't, and adjust the seasoning with salt, pepper, and lemon juice. Stir in the parsley and serve. If reheating, you may need to add extra liquid.

Squid-ink spaghetti with sun-blushed tomatoes

Serves 4   *15 minutes preparation: 15 minutes cooking*

Move over sun-dried tomatoes; there's a new kid on the block and it has various names. Sun-kissed or sun-blushed tomatoes have been slowly roasted in the oven until they are half dried and then submerged in olive oil. They are easy enough to make at home, left in the oven for an hour or two, but it's so convenient to have a store-bought jar in the pantry for impromptu suppers like this one. These tomatoes succeed because they are instantly ready for use in risotto, pasta dishes, salads, and tarts, imparting a similar concentrated tomato flavor to sun-dried but being soft and juicy without the need for rehydration. Non-vegetarians will love the inky black squid-ink spaghetti, which makes this simple but delicious pasta supper stunning to look at—red, green, and white against the black—and the hint of seafood complements the flavors. It is good too with ordinary spaghetti. Any leftovers are delicious warm or cold and perfect for the lunch box.

14oz/400g spaghetti
2 large garlic cloves
3 tbsp olive oil
3oz/85g piece Parmesan cheese

9oz/250g jar sun-blushed or sun-kissed tomatoes
  in olive oil
3oz/85g arugula
salt and freshly ground black pepper

Put a large pan of water on to boil. Salt generously and add the spaghetti. Boil for 10–15 minutes, or until just *al dente*. Drain. Meanwhile, crush the garlic with your fist and flake away the papery skin. Split the cloves lengthwise and remove and discard the green germ growing in the middle. Chop the garlic, then sprinkle with a little salt and use the flat of a knife to work it to a paste.

Pour the olive oil into the spaghetti pan, then stir in the garlic and return to the heat, stirring constantly for about 30 seconds, or until aromatic but uncolored. Add the tomatoes and their olive oil and stir around to heat through, then remove the pan from the heat.

Return the pasta and stir well. Cut the Parmesan cheese into flakes using a potato peeler, then add the arugula and Parmesan to the pan. Season with black pepper and toss again, until the arugula wilts and the Parmesan melts. Serve immediately.

Toasted seed coleslaw

Serves 2   *20 minutes preparation: 3 minutes cooking*

There is something immensely virtuous about raw food. I'm not talking here about steak tartare or sushi; I mean all those healthy crunchy foods like vegetables, nuts, grains, seeds, and sprouts. For me, a week of this sort of raw food is a way to diet without dying of boredom. I can eat, for example, variations on gazpacho until the cows come home. And I love big salads like this one that have enough interesting ingredients to tantalize the taste buds. This healthy detox regime is also a very good reason to treat yourself to a new cook's knife for all the chopping you'll be doing. I admit the traditional mayonnaise-based dressing is hardly low-cal, and here I've added zing with a hint of raw garlic and Dijon mustard. Extra flavor comes from a dollop of crunchy peanut butter. This salad will keep, covered, in the refrigerator for several days.

1 garlic clove
3 tbsp mayonnaise
1 heaped tsp Dijon mustard
2 tbsp lemon juice
1 tbsp toasted sesame oil
1 scant tbsp crunchy peanut butter
1 small white or red cabbage, about 1lb/500g

2 medium carrots
3 scallions
1 crisp eating apple
2oz/55g pumpkin or sunflower seeds or 1oz/25g
   of each
1oz/25g sesame seeds
salt and freshly ground black pepper

Peel and chop the garlic. Sprinkle with salt, then use the flat of a knife to work to a juicy paste. Transfer to a salad bowl and stir in the mayonnaise followed by the mustard. Now stir in 1 tablespoon of the lemon juice and then the sesame oil. Work the peanut butter into the mixture.

Cut the cabbage into fourths lengthwise and cut out the solid stem. Finely shred the cabbage across the segments. Peel the carrots and grate. Trim the scallions and slice on the slant in super-thin slices. Peel the apple and cut into fourths, then core and chop. As you chop, toss the apple immediately with the remaining lemon juice. Stir the cabbage, carrots, scallions, and apple into the dressing. Season with black pepper.

Heat a skillet and, when hot, stir-fry the pumpkin seeds until they begin to pop and the skins crack. Tip onto a plate. Add the sesame seeds to the pan and stir until pale golden. Add both seeds to the salad. Toss again and serve.

Tumbet

Serves 2–4   *35 minutes preparation: 60 minutes cooking*

Without sounding dramatic, I do beg you to make this Majorcan vegetable casserole. I came across the recipe while I was looking for insight into Majorcan cooking. Authentic Majorcan recipes come with a stern warning that the dish relies on the quality of the raw ingredients. No doubt it is superb when made with Majorcan eggplants (claimed to be the best in the world), bell peppers, and potatoes, but my version made with supermarket vegetables was out of this world. It can be served hot or at room temperature and is great for barbecues and al fresco meals. I have bent the one-pot rule slightly to keep the cooking time down.

2 eggplants
4 large garlic cloves
6 ripe plum tomatoes
olive oil

1 sprig fresh marjoram or oregano or tsp dried
2 large potatoes, scrubbed
4 red bell peppers
salt and freshly ground black pepper

Trim the eggplants and slice into ½–1in/1–2.5cm circles. Spread them out on several sheets of absorbent paper towels and salt well, then weight them with a heavy plate or baking dish for 30 minutes. Pat the slices dry with the paper towels, brushing off the excess salt.

Meanwhile, peel and finely chop the garlic. Place the tomatoes in a bowl, then cover with boiling water and count to 20. Drain, then cut out the cores in a small cone shape and remove the skin. Cut the tomatoes into fourths, then scrape out the seeds and chop the flesh. Sauté the garlic briefly in a small amount of oil, then add the tomatoes and marjoram and cook, covered, over low heat for 20 minutes, or until thick and sauce-like. Salt to taste.

At the same time, cut the unpeeled potatoes into ½in/1cm slices and sauté slowly in batches in about ¼in/5mm of oil until golden brown, removing and draining on paper towels when done. Arrange the slices in the bottom of a flameproof dish. Cut the stems out of the bell peppers and cut the bell peppers into fourths, then discard the pale inner ridges and wash away the seeds. Cut into ½in/1cm slices. Cook the bell peppers in the remaining potato oil until slippery and soft and browned in places. What seems an impossibly large amount will flop down considerably. Transfer to absorbent paper towels to drain.

Finally, cook the eggplant slices slowly, turning often, adding more oil as necessary, until soft and golden brown. Remove and drain, then arrange them on top of the potato slices. Place the bell peppers on top and pour over the tomato sauce. Cover the dish snugly with a double fold of aluminum foil and cook over low heat for 15 minutes. This can also be done in the oven—cooking, covered, at 350°F/180°C. Let stand, covered, for 5–10 minutes before serving, or cool to room temperature.

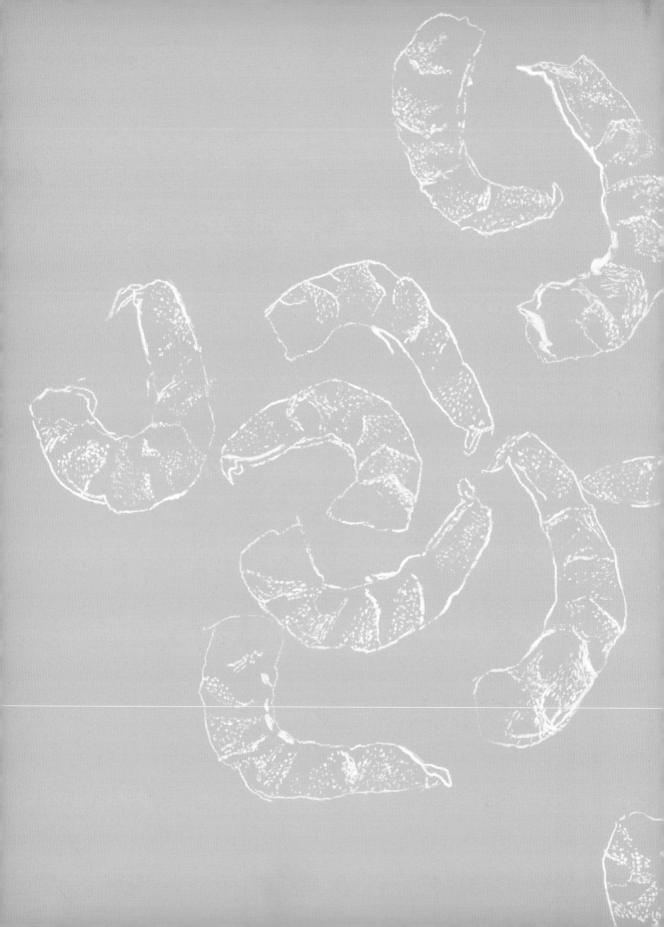

Seafood

Whenever television chefs proclaim the virtues of seafood and show us how to cook it, my fish dealer does a roaring trade. On Friday—traditionally the British day for a fish supper—business is brisk and on Saturday, when the men folk go shopping, he sells more luxury seafood such as wild salmon, halibut and langoustine. The rest of the week, whatever the time of year, business is up and down. It's rare to see the sort of queues that are commonplace at the butcher.

Every day, bar Monday when most fish shops are closed, he lays out his display on the wet slab like a work of art. He orders his fish alphabetically, he tells me, before rattling off the briny litany of today's catch, but his display is a matter of what takes his fancy. Slippery, plump, pointed angler fish tails might line up next to handsome golden gray soles or orange-spotted plaice. Stupendous whole codfish usually snuggle up to neatly sliced fillets and oval-shaped steaks that show the huge flakes of this dense, succulent fish. The mottled green-gray and golden skins of herrings, sardines, and mackerel glint beguilingly next to the stupendous sight of a large salmon trout or a startlingly pink salmon tail. Less familiar fish, such as hoki and tilapia, and unfashionable huss (also known as many as dog fish, wolf fish, or rock fish), look ordinary next to huge steaks of burgundy-red tuna. These in turn appear spookily unfishy against a neat pile of snowy-white squid, their tentacles alarmingly alien to many customers. In the shellfish corner there might be brown and pink shrimp, mounds of blue-black mussels, and dressed crab, the white and brown meat neatly separated and laid out in its shell. Often there are unfamiliar spider crabs, their huge, knobbly bodies resting on long, folded legs. Occasionally a browny-blue live lobster or crayfish, its claws safely ensnared in wide, blue rubber bands, sleepily surveys the scene. When there's an "r" in the month, native oysters spill out of their traditional wooden barrel.

For customers like me, these displays are endlessly tempting. Part of the pleasure of these visits is watching my fish dealer choose a knife from his razor-sharp collection and with deft efficiency do whatever is necessary to render my choice ready for the pan. He decorates his piscatorial display with colorful plastic lobsters, fishnets, and buoys. These are popular with small children, who drag their mothers to the window and occasionally into the shop to get closer to the lobsters' faceted carapace and long, whiskery antennae.

The basic rule when buying fish, wherever it's from, is to look for bright, plump eyes, clear skin that is hard to the touch, a clean smell, and bright red gills.

Fillets should feel firm, look clean, and smell unfishy. Shellfish should have tightly shut shells and feel heavy and full. Whether your fish comes from a fish dealer (often family-run and with knowledgeable staff) or the supermarket (which has keen prices due to buying power but no specialty staff), it provides the perfect solution for the cook in a hurry, who wants a healthy, nutritious meal. It is easy to cook in a variety of ways—poached, steamed, baked, stewed, and fried—and offers a huge choice of textures and flavors. All fish, particularly oily fish like mackerel and tuna, are a good source of omega-3 fatty acids. These polyunsaturated fats make the blood less likely to clot, so people who eat fatty fish regularly have a lower risk of heart attack. It's also a good source of vitamins A and D, which strengthen hair, bones, and teeth.

There is only one rule to remember about cooking fish: don't overcook.

After-work bouillabaisse

Serves 3–4 *15 minutes preparation: 20 minutes cooking*

It's the devil of a palaver to make a real bouillabaisse. The Mediterranean fisherman's soup was traditionally prepared with fish left behind in the nets, but has ended up being a soup of romance and mystery surrounded by legend and hearsay. This basic version dispenses with the elaborate fish stock, but includes the saffron which gives the soup its distinctive aroma and flavor, not to mention a yellow color. Any firm white fish is perfect, and a mixture would be just dandy. The shrimp add color and a welcome change of texture. This big soup is healthy and low in calories. For a perfectly balanced meal, serve it with a handful of lightly cooked green beans.

12 medium-size waxy variety or new potatoes
1 onion
2 garlic cloves
2 tbsp olive oil
1 large fennel bulb
3 plum tomatoes
strip orange zest measuring 2in x ½in/5cm x 1cm

½ chicken stock cube
pinch saffron
14oz/400g cod, haddock, pollock, or other thick,
  firm white fish fillets
6oz/175g raw or cooked jumbo shrimp
small bunch of flatleaf parsley
salt and freshly ground black pepper

Put the unpeeled potatoes on to boil in plenty of salted water. When tender to the point of a knife, drain the potatoes, then return to the pan and cover with cold water. Let stand for about 1 minute to cool, then drain again and remove the skins. Halve the potatoes. Meanwhile, peel and finely chop the onion. Peel the garlic, then chop coarsely and sprinkle with ½ teaspoon salt. Crush in a pestle and mortar or using the flat of a knife to make a juicy paste.

Heat the oil in a large skillet or similarly wide-based pan and stir in the onion and garlic. Sauté gently, stirring often, for about 5 minutes without letting the onion brown. Split the fennel bulb and cut out the dense core, then slice across the layers very finely, reserving the fronds. Add the fennel to the onion, increase the heat slightly and cook for 5 minutes more.

Meanwhile, pour boiling water over the tomatoes and count to 20, then drain and remove the skin. Chop the tomatoes. Add the tomatoes, orange zest, and a generous pinch of salt to the pan together with a generous grinding of black pepper. Let the vegetables simmer gently for 6–7 minutes, or until almost soft. Dissolve the stock cube in 1½ cups boiling water and stir in the saffron. Pour onto the vegetables and bring to a boil.

Simmer for a couple of minutes while you slice the fish into 1in/2.5cm wide chunks. Check the seasoning of the liquids, then slip in the pieces of fish so they are covered. Cook for 2–3 minutes, or until the fish has turned white and opaque. Add the shrimp and potatoes and warm through. If using raw shrimp, cook slightly longer until bright pink. Chop the fennel fronds and parsley leaves, then sprinkle over the top of the soup and serve.

Clams with tomato and linguine

Serves 4   *25 minutes preparation: 20 minutes cooking*

Lido Azzurro is a modest but spectacularly located seafood restaurant on Italy's Amalfi coast. The dishes are simple, relying on the best and freshest ingredients, and the service is friendly and efficient. This was my first encounter with coal-black squid-ink bread, a wonderful trend just waiting to happen elsewhere. Imagine serving your crostini and bruschetta on black toast piled with snowy mozzarella and slippery roasted red bell peppers. I loved the simplicity of tossing baby shrimps with arugula, lemon juice, and olive oil and seasoning crab with nothing more than lemon juice and grassy olive oil. This is my interpretation of a clam soup from this charming place. They serve it with lightly toasted bread to dip into the juices.

2lb/1kg clams
14oz/400g linguine
1 tbsp olive oil
1 onion
4 garlic cloves
1 red chile

1oz/25g bunch flatleaf parsley
1lb/500g vine tomatoes
½ stick butter
1 tsp chopped thyme
1¼ cups white wine
salt and freshly ground black pepper

Place the clams in a sink full of cold water and agitate with your hands. Use a nail brush to give each one a quick but thorough scrub. Drain away the water, then refill the sink and agitate again. Drain and rinse until the water runs clean. Scoop the clams into a colander to drain. Discard any that remain open after tapping with a knife.

Put a large pan of water on to boil for the pasta and cook according to the package directions. Drain, then toss with the olive oil and return to a large, warmed bowl. Cover and keep warm. Meanwhile, peel and finely chop the onion and garlic. Trim and split the chile and scrape away the seeds. Slice the halves into skinny strips and then chop into tiny dice. Coarsely chop the parsley. Pour boiling water over the tomatoes. Count to 20, then drain and splash with cold water. Remove the skins and cut into fourths, then scrape away the seeds and chop the flesh.

Melt ¼ stick of the butter in the pan placed over medium-low heat. Add the garlic, onion, chile, and thyme and cook, stirring frequently, adjusting the heat as necessary, for 6–7 minutes, or until the onions are soft but not browned. Add the clams and wine. Increase the heat, then cover the pan and boil for about 3 minutes, or until all the clams open. Discard any that remain closed. Remove the clams with a slotted spoon and keep to one side.

Reduce the liquid in the pan by half by boiling hard without a lid. Lower the heat, then add the tomato dice and stir in the remaining butter. Stir the clams into the hot sauce, then tip into the pasta. Add the parsley and season with salt and black pepper, then toss and serve.

Cod with white beans

Serves 2   *15 minutes preparation: 25 minutes cooking*

I feel a twinge of guilt every time I suggest a recipe using cod, particularly after headlines predicting its disappearance from the North Sea due to over-fishing. Some of the finest cod I've eaten recently came from Norway. It's fished in the deep, clear waters of the Barents Sea above the Arctic Circle and careful management and advanced fishing techniques mean the supply is reliable and consistent. It's noticeable for the thick, large fillets which fall into the characteristically big flakes of dense pearly white fish when cooked. Dishes like this show the incredible versatility of cod. Be sure not to overcook it; the minute the flesh turns opaque and comes away easily with your fork, it's ready.

3 strips rindless lean bacon
1 tbsp cooking oil
1 medium onion
14oz/400g canned cannellini or Great Northern
  beans
1 large garlic clove
1 lemon

½ chicken stock cube
Tabasco sauce
2 tomatoes, preferably plum
handful flatleaf parsley
9oz/250g thick cod, haddock, or pollock fillet
salt and freshly ground black pepper

Slice across the bacon strips to make little strips. Heat the oil in a medium-size heavy-bottom pan and cook the bacon until crisp. Peel and finely chop the onion. Add it to the bacon and cook for 5–6 minutes, or until tender and lightly browned.

Tip the beans into a strainer, then rinse with cold water and shake dry. Peel the garlic and chop it very finely. Remove the lemon zest in wafer-thin sheets and chop very finely. Stir this and the garlic into the pan and cook for a minute or so until aromatic. Add the beans and season generously with pepper and lightly with salt. Dissolve the stock cube in 1 cup boiling water to make the stock. Add it and a generous splash of Tabasco to the pan. Simmer briskly for 5 minutes.

Meanwhile, cover the tomatoes with boiling water and count to 20, then drain and peel. Coarsely chop the parsley. Cut the fish into big bite-size chunks and season with salt and pepper. Stir the tomatoes and most of the parsley into the beans. Cook for an additional 2 minutes, then stir in the fish, making sure it's all submerged. Cook for 5–10 minutes, or until the fish is opaque.

Check the seasoning: you may need a little more Tabasco or a squeeze of lemon and extra salt and pepper. Serve in shallow soup bowls with the last of the parsley and a wedge of lemon.

Cod with tomatoes, bell peppers, and black olives

Serves 2 *15 minutes preparation: 20 minutes cooking*

If using frozen cod fillets for this light yet deliciously satisfying quick fish supper, a useful tip is to sprinkle the defrosted fish with a little salt and let it stand for a few minutes before cooking. This has the double effect of drawing out excess water and firming up the fish. It also means the fish is seasoned right through the fillet. I love this sauce-cum-salsa and thick flakes of creamy cod with crusty bread, but rice or, if you prefer, boiled or mashed potato with lightly cooked green beans would be good too.

2 cod steaks or large fillets, about 9oz/250g
1 large red onion
1 plump garlic clove
3 tbsp olive oil
3oz/85g roasted red bell pepper from a jar
12oz/375g tomatoes

1 tbsp tomato paste
8 pitted black olives
handful flatleaf parsley
flour for dusting
salt and freshly ground black pepper

If using frozen cod steaks, let defrost or speed things up by soaking in cold water for about 10 minutes. Peel and halve the onion, then finely chop. Peel the garlic and slice in super-thin circles. Heat 2 tablespoons of the oil in a skillet and, when very hot, stir in the onion and garlic. Cook, stirring often, for at least 5 minutes, adjusting the heat so that the onion softens without crisping.

Meanwhile, slice the red bell pepper into ribbons and then into short strips. Pour boiling water over the tomatoes. Count to 20 and drain, then cut out the core and remove the skin. Coarsely chop the tomatoes. Stir the tomatoes and red bell pepper into the onion. Season generously with salt and pepper, then stir in the tomato paste and cook for 5 minutes. Tear the olives into 2 or 3 pieces each and stir them in too, cooking for an additional couple of minutes. Taste and adjust the seasoning. Coarsely chop the parsley and stir into the sauce. Transfer the sauce to a bowl and keep warm.

Give the fish a gentle squeeze to remove excess water. Pat dry on absorbent paper towels. Dust the fish with flour and shake away any excess. Heat the remaining oil in the pan and, when hot, quickly cook the fish for about 30 seconds a side. Spoon the sauce over the fish in the pan and heat through, then divide between two warmed plates.

Crab and cucumber linguine

Serves 4–6   *20 minutes preparation: 15 minutes cooking*

White crab meat simply dressed with lemon juice, olive oil, and chopped flatleaf parsley is a wonderful combination. It makes a deliciously indulgent home-alone supper piled onto bruschetta made by toasting thick slices of sourdough bread, rubbing it with garlic, and generously smearing it with olive oil. A good addition, which makes the crab go farther and lends a crisp, clean flavor and crunchy texture, is thin slices of peeled and seeded cucumber. Adding a few scraps of finely chopped red chile lifts the flavors in an exciting and delicious way. If you want to share your feast with friends, the crab mixture is terrific when mixed into hot linguine. Linguine is the pasta of the moment and, although it is similar to spaghetti, its firmer texture and thinner strands give exactly the right sort of resistance to the bite against the silky-white crab meat and thin slices of peeled cucumber which wilt against its heat. Serve this lovely summer pasta supper with a glass of chilled white wine. It is rich and luscious; do not be tempted to serve it with Parmesan or any other grated cheese.

14oz/400g linguine
1 tsp dried red chili flakes or 2 fresh red chiles
1 small or ½ large cucumber
2 large dressed crabs and 6 large claws, yielding
    about 9oz/250g brown meat and 7oz/200g white

juice of 2 large lemons
2 tbsp coarsely chopped flatleaf parsley
6–8 tbsp extra virgin olive oil
sea salt and freshly ground black pepper

Put a large pan of water on to boil. Cook the pasta until it is *al dente*, then drain and return to the pan. Meanwhile, place the chili flakes in an egg cup and just cover with boiling water, then let stand for a few minutes until soft. If using fresh chiles, trim and split them, scraping away the seeds. Slice into skinny strips and then into tiny dice.

Remove the skin from the cucumber with a potato peeler. Split it in half lengthwise and use a teaspoon to scrape out the seeds and their watery surround. Thinly slice the cucumber into half moons. In a bowl, mix together the drained chili flakes or fresh chile, dressed crab, juice from 1½ of the lemons, and the chopped parsley and season lightly with salt and generously with pepper. Crack the crab claws and scrape the meat off the flat central "bone," leaving it in big chunks, directly into the mixture. Slowly stir in 4 tablespoons of the olive oil to make a thick but slack mixture.

Stir the cucumber and 2 tablespoons of the olive oil into the drained pasta, stirring to mix thoroughly and encouraging the cucumber to wilt slightly. Now add the crab mixture, adding more lemon juice or oil to taste. Serve with forks and spoons.

Crab jambalaya

Serves 6 *30 minutes preparation: 45 minutes cooking*

My mother-in-law, Betty John, was a terrific cook. She had what they call in Trinidad a "sweet hand," able to make something special out of quite ordinary ingredients and unfazed by unexpected guests. This was one of her specialties that she made regularly with the crabs at her disposal in the Cornish fishing village where she lived. I made it twice recently, both times doing it from scratch, boiling and picking the crabs, then making stock with the remains, using basmati rice on one occasion and risotto rice on another. Proper crab stock obviously gives the dish a superb depth of flavor, and picking the crabs yourself means that the white crab meat can be left in delicious big lumps. This quickie version using dressed crab and stock cubes or a jar of Mediterranean fish soup is pretty good, too, although you might want to buy a few crab claws to add textural interest. Serve the jambalaya risotto-style; I quite like green beans on the side.

2 red onions
2 garlic cloves
2 tbsp vegetable oil
2 red bell peppers
1 bay leaf
3 dried chiles
14oz/400g fresh tomatoes or 14oz/400g canned
   skinless cherry tomatoes
9oz/250g basmati rice

3 dressed crabs, yielding about 9oz/250g brown
   meat and 7oz/200g white
2½ cups chicken or fish stock (cubes are fine)
   or jar Mediterranean fish soup
1 small lemon
Tabasco sauce
salt and freshly ground black pepper
2 tbsp chopped flatleaf parsley

Peel and dice the onions and garlic. Heat the oil in large skillet or similarly wide-based pan and stir in the onions and garlic. Cook gently for 5 minutes or so while you dice the red bell peppers, discarding seeds, white membrane, and stem. Stir the bell peppers into the onions, together with the bay leaf and chiles, cooking for about 15 minutes, or until the onions are soft and slippery, the bell peppers partially softened, and the chiles crumbled.

Meanwhile, rinse the rice in several changes of water. If using fresh tomatoes, place them in a bowl and cover with boiling water. Count to 20 and drain. Remove the skins, then cut out the core and coarsely chop them. Stir the rice into the vegetables in the skillet and then add the brown crab meat. Cook for a couple of minutes, then add the tomatoes and their juices, ½ teaspoon salt, and plenty of pepper. Now add the stock and bring the liquid to a boil. Stir, then reduce the heat and cook, covered, for 15 minutes.

Turn off the heat and leave the skillet without removing the lid—the rice will finish cooking in the steam generated—for 10 minutes. Stir in the white crab meat. Taste the juices, then adjust the seasoning with salt, pepper, and lemon juice, adding a shake or two of Tabasco if it isn't hot enough. Stir in the parsley and serve.

Leek salad with pilchards and balsamic dressing

Serves 2   *10 minutes preparation: 15 minutes cooking*

Pilchards are grown-up sardines and a specialty of Cornwall, England. Sadly, they have never caught on, either canned or fresh, in the same way as sardines or their relative the mackerel, but there are moves afoot to widen the appeal of Cornish pilchards. The canning process has been brought into line with that of the finest sardines and tuna, by first filleting the fish and flash-frying them before they are canned in extra virgin olive oil. If you can find these tasty morsels, they work wonderfully well in this light and healthy salad supper, but if not, tuna fillets work well too. With plenty of crusty bread and butter, the salad is satisfying enough as an entrée, but if you have big appetites, start with soup or finish with a dessert.

2 trimmed leeks, about 10oz/300g

scant 1 cup extra fine green beans

2 eggs, hard-cooked

3½oz/100g canned Cornish pilchard fillets or
   2½oz/65g canned tuna fillets, oil reserved

5oz/150g cherry tomatoes

1 tbsp aged balsamic vinegar

2 tbsp extra virgin olive oil

1 tbsp finely chopped chives

salt and freshly ground black pepper

Cut the leeks into three or four 4in/10cm lengths. Bring a large pan of water to a boil, then salt generously and add the leeks. Return the water to a boil, then cover the pan and boil for about 5 minutes, or until the leeks are cooked through and can be pierced easily with a sharp knife. Scoop the leeks into a colander, upending them to drain and cool. Trim the beans, then cut them in half and add them to the boiling leeks water. Return to a boil and boil for 2–3 minutes, or until just *al dente*. Drain.

Meanwhile, peel the eggs and cut into fourths lengthwise. Halve the tomatoes round their middles. Gently squeeze the leeks to remove any trapped water and remove the outer layer if it seems crusty.

Arrange the leeks on two dinner plates. Cover with a share of the beans and scatter the tomatoes over the top. Arrange the pilchard fillets over the salad and add the eggs. Season with black pepper and balsamic vinegar. Dribble the oil from the fish can over the salad, adding some of the extra virgin olive oil if necessary. Scatter the chives over the top and serve.

Angler fish chowder with green beans and thyme

Serves 2 *20 minutes preparation: 30 minutes cooking*

There couldn't be a much simpler and quicker way of making a comforting and satisfying yet chic and healthy fish supper than this soup-cum-stew. It's roughly based on a New England chowder. These chunky soups usually contain seafood and potatoes and are always made with milk. If you are a meat-eater, a good way of perking up a homely soup like this is with a few scraps of crispy fried bacon. Cook it right at the beginning, then remove when nicely crisped, leaving behind a smoky bacon flavor. Sprinkled over the top with the parsley, it makes a delicious salty garnish. If buying angler fish from a fish dealer, be sure to ask him to remove the slippery membrane that covers the fish fillets, and if buying from a supermarket, check that it has been removed. If left intact, it will shrink and turn horribly rubbery during the cooking. This lovely soup is plenty for two as an entrée and sufficient for four if followed with something else. Serve with crusty bread and butter for dunking.

1lb 6oz/625g new potatoes
1lb/500g angler fish fillet
1 leek, about 4oz/115g
1 shallot
¼ stick butter
1 sprig thyme

1 bay leaf
scant ¾ cup green beans (extra fine if possible)
1¾ cups milk
1 tbsp finely chopped flatleaf parsley
salt and freshly ground black pepper

Boil the unpeeled potatoes in plenty of salted water until tender. Drain and return to the pan, then cover with cold water and let stand for a couple of minutes. Drain again, then remove the skins and cut into chunks. Meanwhile, cut the angler fish into small kabob-size chunks. Trim the leek and split lengthwise, then slice across the leek to make chunky half moons. Tip into a colander, then rinse under cold water and shake dry. Trim, peel and finely chop the shallot.

Melt the butter in a heavy-bottom, lidded pan placed over medium-low heat. Stir in the leek and shallot. Add a generous seasoning of salt and pepper, the thyme, and bay leaf. Adjust the heat so that the vegetables soften gently, then cover the pan and cook for 10 minutes. Trim the beans, then cut them in half. Stir the beans into the leek and shallot, then cover the pan and cook, stirring a couple of times, for an additional 5 minutes.

Now add the fish. Stir as it firms and turns snowy white. Add the potatoes and milk. Simmer for about 10 minutes to finish cooking the fish. Taste and adjust the seasoning. Remove the thyme and bay leaf, then sprinkle with the chopped parsley and serve.

Pan-fried salmon tabbouleh

Serves 6   *30 minutes preparation: 10 minutes cooking*

Tabbouleh is the name of a Lebanese cracked wheat salad with a high proportion of flatleaf parsley and tomatoes. In this salmon version, big chunks of crusty pan-fried salmon are folded into the olive-oil-and-lemon-tossed salad, together with a handful of young spinach, some mint, and finely sliced scallions. It is extremely simple to make and tastes as lively and attractive as it looks. As with most cracked wheat and couscous salads, it doesn't matter a jot if some ingredients are hot and others are warm or cold.

6oz/175g bulgur cracked wheat
4 firm vine tomatoes, approx 14oz/400g
4oz/125g scallions
juice 1 lemon
½ cup olive oil

1 large bunch flatleaf parsley, at least 3oz/85g
large handful mint leaves
generous 1 cup small young spinach leaves
4 fresh salmon fillets, skinned
salt and freshly ground black pepper

Boil the kettle and measure off 1¼ cups water into a mixing bowl. Add the bulgur. Cover the dish and let soak for 15 minutes while you place a strainer over a bowl and cut the tomatoes into fourths lengthwise. Scrape the seeds and juices into the strainer. Using the back of a spoon, press the seeds and juices against the side of the strainer to extract the maximum juice.

Coarsely chop the tomatoes. Trim and finely slice the scallions. Whisk together the tomato juice, lemon juice, and olive oil. Season generously with salt and pepper and stir the mixture into the bulgur. Stir in the scallions and then the tomatoes. Pick the leaves off the parsley stems and chop. Shred the mint leaves. Stir both into the bulgur. Add the spinach and stir again.

Now cook the salmon. Heat a nonstick skillet over medium heat. If you wish, paint the fish with a little cooking oil, although the heat will release the fish's natural oils. Arrange the salmon in the skillet. Cook for 2 minutes a side, pressing down to encourage crusty edges and until just cooked but still moist. Lift out of the skillet and let cool. Flake the fish into ragged chunks. Gently mix the fish into the salad and serve.

Mussels with coconut cream, chile, and cilantro

Serves 2–4   *15 minutes preparation: 20 minutes cooking*

As a general rule, the time to eat oysters and mussels is when there is an "r" in the month and September is generally regarded as the start of the season. Dealing with oysters is best left to the experts, but preparing mussels is child's play. These days their beautiful black-blue shells come relatively clean and they are ready for the pot in minutes. This is a Thai-style take on moules marinière *and the resultant broth has the hallmarks of a coconut-milk Thai soup, being all at once creamy, sour, chile-hot, and citrus-scented. Serve with crusty bread; I think there is plenty here for four big appetites, but the mussels are very more-ish.*

4lb/2kg mussels
1 red onion
1 small unwaxed lemon
3 garlic cloves
2 small red chiles

2 tbsp vegetable oil
2 tbsp Thai fish sauce (*nam pla*)
generous ¾ cup coconut cream
2oz/55g bunch cilantro
freshly ground black pepper

Tip the mussels into a sink of cold water and agitate thoroughly, repeating a few times until the water runs clean. Discard any mussels that are cracked or open. Pull off the "beards" and discard. Leave the mussels in a colander to finish draining while you prepare the broth. Peel and halve the onion, then finely chop. Using a zester or potato peeler, remove the zest from half the lemon in paper-thin strips and chop quite small. Peel and finely chop the garlic. Trim and split the chiles and scrape away the seeds, then slice into thin strips and across into tiny scraps. Don't forget to wash your hands to remove the chile juice, which burns sensitive areas.

Heat the oil in a large pan with a well-fitting lid. Stir in the onion, lemon zest, garlic, and chile and cook, adjusting the heat so nothing burns, for 6–7 minutes, or until the onion is tender. Add the fish sauce, coconut cream, and juice from half of the lemon. Season generously with black pepper. Chop the cilantro, including the stems, which should be sliced very finely, and add half of the bunch (including stems) to the pan. Simmer for a couple of minutes, then taste and adjust the seasoning with lemon juice.

Tip the drained mussels into the pan and stir a couple of times with a wooden spoon, then clamp on the lid and cook at high heat for 5 minutes. Lift off the lid to check if the mussels are opening—it doesn't take long—and then give the pan a good shake or another stir, trying to bring the already opened mussels on the bottom to the top. Replace the lid and cook for a few more minutes. Check again that all the mussels are open, returning the lid for a couple more minutes if necessary. Add the rest of the cilantro and give a final stir, then tip the contents of the pan into a warmed bowl. Discard any mussels which haven't opened.

Pad Thai

Serves 4   *15 minutes preparation: 10 minutes cooking*

Pad Thai is the noodle dish that everyone loves—and a good one, when the noodles are silky and moist with their delicious garlicky, sweet-and-sour sauce, and the pile is well-loaded with shrimp and other tidbits. My version is generous with the chopped peanuts, cilantro, and sliced scallion, with several wedges of lime or lemon. You can probably buy everything you need at the supermarket but, if you are lucky enough to have one nearby, it is much more fun shopping for the authentic ingredients at a Thai store, and the families who run them tend to be so charming and helpful.

7oz/200g medium egg noodles
3 tbsp sweet chili sauce
3 tbsp Thai fish sauce (*nam pla*)
3 tbsp vegetable oil
3 large garlic cloves
7oz/200g raw headless jumbo shrimp or cooked
  peeled large shrimp
7fl oz/200ml carton coconut cream

½ tbsp shrimp paste
2 large eggs
2 scallions
2 tbsp salted roasted peanuts
generous 1¼ cups bean sprouts
2 tbsp cilantro leaves
2 limes or lemons, cut into wedges

As always with a stir-fry, get everything laid out and ready, preferably in the order that it is going to hit the pan, before you start cooking. Place the noodles in large pan and cover with boiling water. Return to a boil, then let soak for 4 minutes. Drain and toss with the chili sauce mixed with the fish sauce and 1 tablespoon of the oil. Peel and finely chop the garlic. If using raw shrimp, peel them but leave the tail ends intact. Run a sharp knife down their curled backs, cutting less than halfway through.

Heat the coconut cream and shrimp paste in a small pan, stirring until smooth and hot. Add the raw or cooked shrimp. If using raw shrimp, cook gently for a couple of minutes, or until pink and cooked through. Whisk the eggs in a bowl with ½ tablespoon of the oil. Finely slice the scallions on the slant. Coarsely grind the peanuts in a blender or food processor.

Heat the wok and add the remaining oil, swirling it round the pan. Add the garlic, cooking for about 30 seconds, or until golden. Add the eggs, letting them set, then stir to scramble. Add the noodles and toss and stir for a couple of minutes. Add the shrimp and coconut mix, tossing thoroughly and breaking down the scrambled egg against the noodles and shrimp. Add the bean sprouts and stir-fry until barely cooked.

Pile the Pad Thai onto a platter and strew with the scallions, cilantro leaves, and peanuts. Edge with the lime wedges and serve.

Potato gnocchi with shrimp and minted peas

Serves 2 *10 minutes preparation: 15 minutes cooking*

This classy little number is the perfect smart comfort supper for two. It ends up risotto-like, the starch from the gnocchi slightly thickening the white-wine juices. It is similarly more-ish and very satisfying. Serve it with ciabatta or another crusty bread and some decent butter. Drink the rest of the bottle of wine with the meal.

14oz/400g ready-made potato gnocchi
4oz/125g scallions
½ stick butter
1½ cups frozen baby peas
¾ cup white wine

7oz/200g cooked shelled large shrimp
2 tbsp chopped mint
2 tbsp grated Parmesan cheese
salt and freshly ground black pepper

Put a large skillet or similar-size wide-based pan of water on to boil. Add the gnocchi and plenty of salt and return to a boil. The gnocchi are done when they've all risen to the surface. Drain thoroughly.

Trim and finely slice the scallions. Melt the butter in the skillet and soften the scallions. After about 5 minutes, add the frozen peas. Season with salt and pepper and cook for 2–3 minutes, or until the peas are tender and the scallions very soft. Add the white wine and stir well, then return the gnocchi. Bubble steadily for several minutes to reduce slightly and infuse the gnocchi with the flavor, then stir in the shrimp.

Cook until the shrimp are hot. Taste and adjust the seasoning with salt and pepper, then stir in the chopped mint. Dust with the Parmesan and serve.

Caesar salad with smoked salmon

Serves 2   *15 minutes preparation: 5 minutes cooking*

One of the most popular lunch dishes at the Porthgwidden Beach Café in St Ives, Cornwall, on one of the hottest days of summer was Caesar salad with smoked salmon. All around me, as I picked my way through the limited menu which had been reduced by a freak power cut, there were people tucking into deep, white bowls full of tall, pointy leaves draped with smoked salmon. I copied the idea at home and also made it very successfully with flaked honey-roast Scottish salmon. I cheated with the dressing and stirred anchovy paste into mayonnaise let down with olive oil and wine vinegar, but made my own chunky and very crusty croutons. I copied the Café and included a few strips of prosciutto and flakes of Parmesan—easy to achieve by taking a potato peeler to a chunk of Parmesan. Serve it with crusty bread and butter.

4 slices ciabatta bread or 8 slices baguette
4 tbsp olive oil
1 tbsp mayonnaise
1 tbsp anchovy paste
½ tbsp red wine vinegar

2 baby Romaine lettuces or 4 Boston lettuce hearts
4oz/125g honey-roast salmon flakes or
    5oz/150g smoked salmon trimmings
2 slices prosciutto
10 Parmesan cheese flakes

Cut the bread into postage-stamp-size pieces without removing the crusts. Heat 3 tablespoons of the oil in a skillet and, when hot, add the bread, immediately tossing it around so that all the pieces get a share of oil. Cook briskly until golden on both sides. Tip out onto paper towels to drain.

Place the mayonnaise in a deep salad bowl. Stir in the anchovy paste, remaining olive oil, and red wine vinegar, adding 1 tablespoon water if it seems too thick. Separate the lettuce leaves, then rinse and shake dry. Stir the lettuce into the dressing. Add the flaked fish or scraps of smoked salmon, the prosciutto torn into strips, the Parmesan flakes, and drained croutons. Toss again. Serve immediately.

Squid or scallop provençale with basmati rice

Serves 2–4   *15 minutes preparation: 15 minutes cooking*

*This is a sure-fire winner of a recipe and makes the perfect quick and healthy spring supper.
If you are not sure about squid, try it with shrimp or, if money is no object, scallops. Another
option would be mussels, but these would have to be cooked first, then removed from their shells.
Alternatively, it can be made with firm-fleshed fish such as angler fish. I find it tricky to predict
how many the dish will feed because it is so easy to eat that everyone wants more than expected.*

1½ cups basmati rice
14oz/400g cleaned squid or scallops without shells
2 garlic cloves
9oz/250g cherry tomatoes
½ stick butter

1 tbsp olive oil
1½ lemons (½ for juice, 1 for wedges)
½ glass dry white wine
large bunch flatleaf parsley, at least 3oz/85g
salt and freshly ground black pepper

Rinse the rice until the water runs clean and place in a pan with a well-fitting lid with 1¾ cups
cold water. Bring to a boil, then reduce the heat to very low and cook, covered, for 10 minutes.
Remove from the heat but leave the lid in place for an additional 10 minutes so the rice
finishes cooking in the steam.

Meanwhile, prepare the squid by slicing the sacs in chunky rings, approximately ½in/1cm wide.
Squeeze out the hard mouth from the center of the tentacles—it will pop out easily—and
discard it with everything else. Divide the tentacles into 2 or 3 pieces each, depending on
their size. If using scallops, separate the coral and slice the white part into rounds. Peel and
chop the garlic, then sprinkle with a generous pinch of salt and use the flat of a knife to crush
to a juicy paste. Cut the cherry tomatoes into fourths, then slice across the segments.

Heat the butter and oil in a spacious skillet, then stir in the garlic and almost immediately
the squid or scallops (if using scallops, add the coral for a minute first before adding the rest),
moderating the heat so it cooks gently. After a couple of minutes, squeeze in the juice from
the half lemon and then add the white wine. Let everything bubble up and add the tomatoes.
Cook for 2–3 minutes to allow everything to mix and merge.

Pick the leaves off the parsley and coarsely chop; you need at least 4 heaped tablespoons.
Stir the parsley into the dish before the tomatoes have had a chance to collapse. Season
generously with black pepper and lightly with salt. Serve immediately over the rice with lemon
wedges, accompanied by the rice.

Squid with tomatoes and green peas

Serves 2   *20 minutes preparation: 50 minutes cooking*

Few foods provoke such strong feelings, both for and against, as squid. They make people squeamish—the very same people, probably, who wolf down deep-fried calamari rings on their Spanish holiday. This is a pity because the snowy-white tube-like body of this underrated mollusc is tender and sweet and comes without a shell. Most fish dealers will clean squid for you, but it's a painless and simple enough job if your fish supplier can't do it. Based on an old favorite recipe of Marcella Hazan's, this is a dish to convert would-be squid haters. It can be made up to 48 hours in advance and is best eaten with crusty bread to scoop up the juices.

1 onion	13oz/375g small squid, fresh or frozen, cleaned
2 garlic cloves	2 cups frozen peas
2 tbsp olive oil	salt and freshly ground black pepper
14oz/400g canned chopped tomatoes	lemon wedges to serve

Peel and halve the onion and garlic, then finely chop. Heat the oil in a heavy-bottom, medium-size pan that can hold all the ingredients. Sauté the onion over medium heat, stirring occasionally, for about 10 minutes, or until it begins to soften and turn golden. Add the garlic and cook for a couple of minutes before adding the tomatoes. Cook at a gentle simmer for about 15 minutes, or until the tomatoes begin to thicken and the onion melts into them to make a cohesive sauce.

Meanwhile, slice the squid sacs (its body) into ½in/1cm-wide rings. Cut off the tentacles. Squeeze out the hard mouth from the center of the tentacles—it will pop out easily—and discard it with everything else. Divide the tentacle clusters in half. Add the rings and tentacles to the pan. Season with salt and pepper and stir well, then cover and cook at a gentle simmer for about 20 minutes, or until the squid is tender. Taste and adjust the seasoning.

Stir in the peas and cook for a few minutes until they are done. If the sauce seems too dry—you want the dish to be juicy rather than wet—add a little water. Serve with lemon wedges.

Shrimp laksa with green beans

Serves 4 *30 minutes preparation: 40 minutes cooking*

The point of Malaysian laksa is its finely balanced sweet, sour, hot, and spicy coconut broth. Into this gorgeous liquor go shrimp, bean sprouts, and other vegetables to give crunch, and the "soup" (which is more of a meal) is served over rice noodles. Traditionally, laksa is made with vermicelli-style rice noodles (sometimes sold as stir-fry rice noodles), but egg noodles are good too. It is a great thing to make when you have friends coming over because all preparation can be done in advance and the last-minute cooking is quick and mindless.

2lb/1kg raw jumbo shrimp, headless with shells on
1 onion
3 plump garlic cloves
1oz/25g fresh gingerroot
3 lemongrass stems
bunch cilantro with roots, at least 3oz/85g
1 Scotch Bonnet chile or 4 small red chiles
6 macadamia nuts or 10 blanched almonds
1½ tsp each of ground coriander, cumin, and turmeric

1 tsp brown sugar
2 limes (one for juice, 1 for wedges)
14oz/400g canned coconut milk
2 tbsp vegetable oil
scant 1 cup trimmed French beans
7oz/200g dried stir-fry rice noodles
1⅔ cups bean sprouts
4oz/125g bunch scallions
salt

If using frozen shrimp, soak them in warm water to defrost. Drain, then remove the shells and run a sharp knife down the back of each shrimp to remove the black "vein." Place the shells in a pan with scant 3 cups water and simmer for 15 minutes. Discard the shells and simmer for 5 more minutes. Transfer the stock to a bowl or pitcher.

While the stock is cooking, peel and chop the onion, garlic, and ginger. Peel the lemongrass to locate the tender inner shoot, then chop. Remove 6 coriander roots with 2in/5cm of stem from the bunch. Place these prepared ingredients into the bowl of the food processor. Split and deseed, then chop the chiles. Add the chile, nuts, ground coriander, cumin, turmeric, sugar, 1 teaspoon salt, the juice of 1 lime, 4 tablespoons of the coconut milk, and the oil to the bowl. Blitz to make a red-flecked, yellow paste.

Refill the stock pan with water and put on to boil. Cut the beans in half and boil for 30 seconds. Scoop the beans out of the pan and set aside. Put the noodles in a bowl and pour over the boiling water. Stir and let the noodles rehydrate according to the package directions.

Simmer the spice paste in a large, heavy-bottom pan for 5 minutes. Gradually incorporate the shrimp stock and remaining coconut milk. Simmer for 5 minutes, then add bean sprouts and shrimp. Cook for 6–10 minutes, or until the shrimp are cooked. Trim and finely slice the scallions and coarsely chop the remaining cilantro leaves. Add the beans, scallions, and chopped cilantro to the laksa. Drain the noodles, then share between deep bowls and spoon over the laksa. Serve with lime wedges.

Smoked mackerel noodles with horseradish cream

Serves 4   *15 minutes preparation: 15 minutes cooking*

When you're whizzing round the supermarket, looking for something quick and easy yet unusual and impressive to make for friends for a weekday supper, smoked mackerel isn't the obvious choice. This fusion of flavors will change your mind: a soy-seasoned broth with onions, carrots, beans, and pickled ginger alongside Chinese noodles and cilantro makes a good backdrop for this meaty and robustly flavored fish. The idea comes from one of my sons, who cooked something similar for me for supper recently. It was so good, I had to have a go myself. Do give it a try; it's simple, the ingredients are easy to shop for, and the dish is very economical. Perfect.

2 onions
3 tbsp vegetable oil
2 garlic cloves
1 small red chile
4 carrots
scant 1 cup fine green beans
1½ chicken stock cubes

3 tbsp soy sauce
9oz/250g medium egg noodles
handful cilantro leaves
2oz/55g pickled sushi ginger (see page 66)
4 smoked mackerel fillets
4 tbsp creamed horseradish
salt

Peel and halve the onions, then finely slice. Heat the oil in a spacious pan over medium heat and stir in the onions. Cook, stirring occasionally, for 5 minutes, or until floppy but not browned. Peel the garlic and slice in wafer-thin circles. Trim the chile and split lengthwise, then scrape away the seeds. Slice into skinny batons and then into tiny dice. Stir the garlic and chile into the onions and cook for a couple of minutes.

Trim and peel the carrots, then slice thinly, cutting on the slant. Stir the carrots into the onions, then season lightly with salt and cook and continue stirring for another couple of minutes. Trim and halve the beans. Dissolve the stock cubes in scant 3 cups boiling water. Add the soy sauce, then pour into the pan. Increase the heat and bring the liquid to a boil. Add the beans to the boiling stock, then return to a boil and cook for 2–3 minutes, or until the beans are just tender.

Co-ordinate cooking the noodles according to the package directions—mine took 4 minutes— to be ready now. Drain. Coarsely chop the cilantro and stir it together with the pickled ginger into the broth. Break the mackerel off its skin in bite-size chunks and add that too, letting it warm through. Serve the noodles in soup bowls, then spoon over the broth with the vegetables and fish and garnish with a dollop of horseradish cream.

Tagliatelle with smoked salmon and chives

Serves 2   *10 minutes preparation: 15 minutes cooking*

Not so long ago, smoked salmon was very posh and the only way we thought of eating it was with brown bread and butter. These days, it is much more common: It's available in packs of all sizes from off-cuts and special sandwich slices to half sides, neatly sliced and laid back in their original shape. It's on sale everywhere and quality, inevitably, is variable. As is increasingly evident with all food, you get what you pay for. As an after-work, quick supper ingredient, it's a godsend. It suits all weather conditions and can be snacky or quickly worked up into more of a meal. Try it, for example, with blinis or hot tortillas with a dollop of sour cream stirred with creamed horseradish and a few strips of crisp pancetta. Or with a simple potato salad tossed with olive oil, white wine vinegar, and lots of chopped dill. It is terrific, too, with pasta. For a super-quickie version of this recipe, just stir sour cream or something similar into cooked pasta, then toss with chives and serve draped with smoked salmon and a lemon wedge.

7oz/200g tagliatelle or fettucine
1 shallot
1 large unwaxed lemon
3½oz/100g smoked salmon or trout
½ stick butter

½ glass dry white wine, about scant ½ cup
scant ½ cup sour cream
small bunch chives
salt and freshly ground black pepper

Cook the tagliatelle or fettucine according to the package directions in plenty of salted boiling water until *al dente*. Drain and return to the pan with a couple of tablespoons of the cooking water. Toss and keep warm.

Meanwhile, peel, then halve and finely chop the shallot. Using a zester or potato peeler, remove the zest from half the lemon in paper-thin strips (reserve the rest for wedges). Chop quite small. Slice the salmon into strips. Melt the butter in a small skillet or pan and stir in the shallot and chopped lemon zest. Cook gently, stirring often, for 5–6 minutes, or until the shallot is tender. Add the wine and boil for a couple of minutes until reduced slightly, then stir in the sour cream. Cook for a couple more minutes and stir in the salmon and most of the chives.

Heat through, then tip the contents of the skillet into the pasta. Season generously with black pepper, then toss well and serve with a garnish of chives and lemon wedges for squeezing on top.

Thai shrimp salad with cucumber

Serves 2   *30 minutes preparation: 5 minutes cooking*

A crisp, vital salad to wake up the taste buds. Serve it alone or with basmati rice.

1 lime
7oz/200g raw headless jumbo shrimp
1 red onion
scant 1 cup green beans
½ large cucumber or 1 small one
2 Boston lettuce hearts
2 lemongrass stems
3 large garlic cloves

3 red chiles
3 tsp fresh tamarind
2 tbsp Thai fish sauce (*nam pla*)
½ tbsp cooking oil
about 30 fresh mint leaves
small handful cilantro leaves
salt

Remove the zest from the lime in paper-thin sheets and set aside. If the shrimp are frozen, slip them into a bowl of warm water and leave for 5–6 minutes to defrost. Remove the shells. Run a sharp knife down the back of each shrimp vein and remove the black membrane within. Place the shrimp in a bowl and squeeze over the lime juice. Toss well so the shrimp are thoroughly seasoned and let stand for 10 minutes, then lift them out of the bowl and transfer to a plate.

Peel and halve the red onion, then finely slice. Mix the slices into the lime juice and let marinate while you prepare the rest of the salad. Boil a medium-size pan of water. Trim and halve the beans. Add salt and the beans to the boiling water, then return to a boil and boil for 2 minutes. Drain and splash with cold water to arrest the cooking. Meanwhile, peel the cucumber and split it in half lengthwise. Scrape out the seeds and the watery pulp and slice across the cucumber to make thin half moons. Unfurl the lettuce, then wash and shake dry.

To make the salad dressing, place half the lime zest in the bowl of a blender. Peel the outer layers of the lemongrass to reveal the tender inner shoot. Chop it coarsely. Flake away the papery skin of the garlic. Trim and split the chiles, then scrape away the seeds and chop coarsely. Add the lemongrass, garlic, and chiles to the lime zest together with the tamarind and fish sauce. Drain the lime juice from the red onions into the bowl. Liquidize to a smooth sauce-cum-dressing. If it seems stiff, add 1 tablespoon cold water. Transfer to a mixing bowl.

Heat the oil in a wok or large skillet over medium heat. Add the shrimp and stir-fry for a couple of minutes until just cooked, turning from gray to pink. Stir the hot shrimp into the dressing. Add the beans and cucumber. Arrange the lettuce leaves on a platter or in a large, shallow bowl. Coarsely chop the mint and cilantro and scatter half over the lettuce. Spoon the shrimp mixture over the top and scatter with the last of the herbs. Serve immediately.

Trout and cucumber noodles with sushi ginger

Serves 2   *15 minutes preparation: 15 minutes cooking*

Sometimes a dish is made by adding an unexpected ingredient. Here it is the idea of including sushi ginger—those wafer-thin, pink-frilled slices of pickled ginger which always accompany sushi—in a noodle and fish dish. This is a quick and easy after-work dish which is healthy and made with inexpensive, accessible ingredients. Cucumber is terrific in slurping noodle dishes, adding a clean, crisp taste and texture which goes well with the slippery noodles. Here it also looks pretty with the pink fish and snowy-white noodles. I used ready-soaked, pale and chunky udon wheat noodles, but any round (as opposed to flat) rice or wheat noodles would be good. Sushi ginger is sold by health-food stores, some supermarkets, and many fish dealers.

½ cucumber
2 scallions
½ chicken stock cube
3 tbsp soy sauce
5oz/150g udon or any round noodles soaked

6 slices pickled sushi ginger
2 fillets rainbow trout
all-purpose flour for dusting
1 tbsp vegetable oil

Use a potato peeler to peel the cucumber. Cut it in half lengthwise and scrape away the seeds and their watery surround with a teaspoon. Slice into chunky half moons. Trim the scallions and then finely slice them. Dissolve the stock cube in 1¼ cups boiling water. Add the soy sauce, cucumber, and scallions to the stock. Cover and let stand for 5 minutes.

At the same time, place the noodles in a separate bowl and cover with boiling water. Let stand for 5 minutes. Drain the noodles and divide between two deep bowls. Strain the stock over the top, then stir the cucumber and scallions into the noodles. Cut the ginger slices in half and add to the broth.

Halve the trout fillets across the middle. Dust both sides with flour, shaking off the excess. Heat the oil in a skillet and, when very hot, add the pieces of fish, skin-side down. Cook for a couple of minutes, or until the skin is crisp, then flip to cook the other side briefly. Lay the fish over the noodles and serve.

Tuna and white bean stew

Serves 4–6 *20 minutes preparation: 40 minutes cooking*

One summer I found myself the happy recipient of a glut of fresh tuna, thanks to a lucky catch by a fisherman friend of the family. I seared it on the grill pan and served it with avocado and tomato salsa, I shaved it sushi-style into wafer-thin slices and we ate it with sticky rice and wasabi, and I had another go at my Thai green curry. I was just beginning to wonder what to do next when the latest edition of Australian Gourmet Traveller *popped through my letterbox. Here I found a heart-warming feature on roasts and casseroles and a delicious-sounding recipe for tuna and white bean stew by Jane Hann. Although the list of ingredients makes it sound complicated, I do urge you to give it a go, because it's no trouble to prepare or eat. This is my slightly adjusted version. Serve it with crusty bread to mop up the delicious juices.*

1 onion
1 fennel bulb
2 tbsp olive oil
1 small red chile
3 canned anchovy fillets
1 large garlic clove
1¼ cups chicken or fish stock (a cube is fine)
about ⅔ cup white wine

14oz/400g canned chopped tomatoes
9oz/250g small potatoes scrubbed
1lb/500g tuna fillet
14oz/400g canned cannellini beans
handful cilantro or basil leaves
best olive oil to serve
salt and freshly ground black pepper

Peel and finely chop the onion. Trim the root end of the fennel, then cut it into fourths lengthwise and slice finely. Heat the oil in a spacious, heavy-bottom pan and stir in the onion and fennel, then cover the pan and cook over medium heat for 5 minutes. Give it a stir and season lightly with salt and pepper, then return the lid and cook for an additional 5 minutes.

Meanwhile, split the chile and scrape away the seeds. then chop finely. Coarsely chop the anchovies. Peel the garlic and chop. Add the chile, anchovies, and garlic to the onion and stir for a couple of minutes. Add the stock and white wine, then bring to a boil and simmer for 5 minutes. Now add the tomatoes and bring to a boil again, then turn down the heat and cover the pan. Cook for 15–20 minutes, or until the fennel is tender.

While it is cooking, cook the potatoes in boiling salted water. Drain and keep warm. Cut the tuna into kabob-size chunks. Tip the beans into a strainer and rinse under cold running water. Add the beans, potatoes, and tuna to the stew and cook for 6–8 minute, or until the tuna is just cooked through. Stir in the cilantro. Serve in warmed bowls with a splash of olive oil.

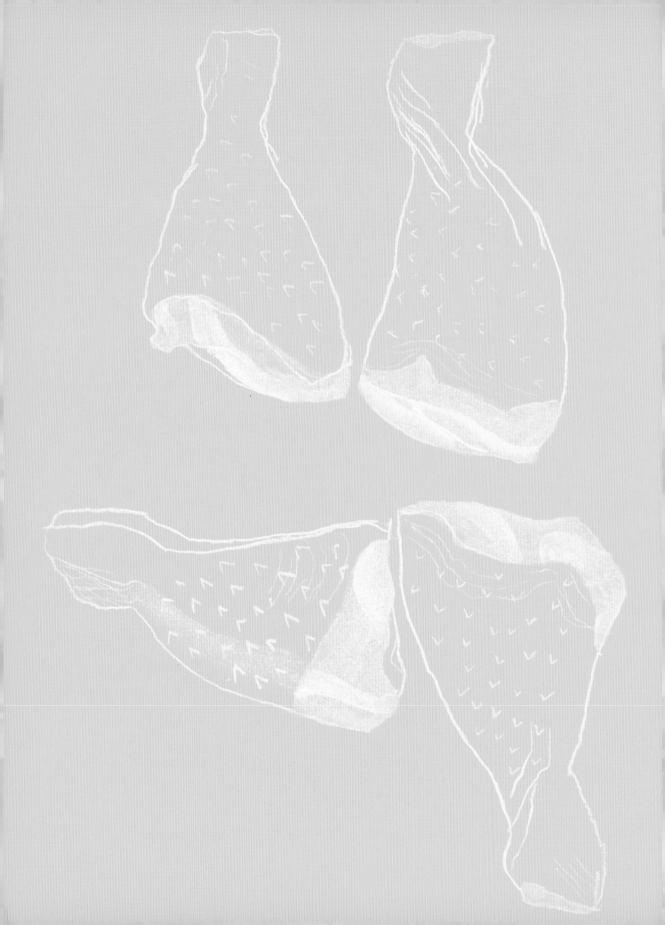

Chicken and duck

Chicken has become crucial to our diet, with sometimes stomach-churning consequences for the birds themselves. Not that long ago, certainly when I was a child growing up in the fifties and sixties, chicken was a treat. Nowadays chicken is a cheap mass-market commodity, and when we want something quick and nourishing for supper, something fresh and easy to turn into a delicious lowfat meal, we turn to chicken, usually chicken breast.

As a general observation about quality, most particularly when it comes to chicken, you get what you pay for. The difference in taste, texture, and size of joints between organically reared chickens and battery-reared broilers is immediately obvious. The fact that organically reared birds take nearly twice as long to mature—12–14 weeks as opposed to six to eight weeks for an ordinary broiler—and are fed a natural diet which isn't laced with hormones, pesticides, and antibiotics is obviously reflected in the price. I'm like most people: I buy those big supermarket trays of chicken portions for the grill, keep a freezer stash of those useful, individually packaged breast fillets which defrost in minutes for "emergencies," but am increasingly likely to pay the extra for organic legs and thighs. I prefer the stronger flavor and the dense, almost chewy texture of these birds. When it comes to buying a whole chicken, I would rather pay almost double the price for quality and eat one less often. These days, supermarkets and butchers all stock organic chicken as a matter of course and also have an abundance of chicken wings and chicken livers in their refrigerators and freezers, which they sell remarkably cheaply. The wings are great for making stock, but are a lip-smacking treat cooked fast and furiously over the grill.

One of the great by-products of a chicken dinner is the bones. With very little effort they can be cooked up into a worthwhile stock. When I wrote *A Celebration of Soup* in the early nineties, I was a stock snob, devoting a big chunk of the book to fine-tuning what I still consider to be a building block of good cooking. A carefully made stock will make some soups, sauces, casseroles, and curries taste richer and more interesting, giving layers of flavor. Over the past ten years or so, stock cubes have improved immeasurably and although I make stock every time I roast or cut up a whole chicken, or bone several legs or thighs (bones, chopped onion, carrot, bay leaf, and any other useful vegetables or herbs are covered with water and left to simmer for a couple of hours, then strained, chilled, and de-fatted before use), I use stock cubes or granules most of the time.

Stock granules, sold in a tub, are brilliant. It's laziness really: you stir a scoop into hot water or directly into whatever you are making and it dissolves like instant coffee. It also avoids all those half-finished cubes that everyone has moldering at the back of the shelf, slowly oozing out of their foil. A can of consommé, which is really superior stock, is another useful standby.

So now you know: when it comes to chicken, you pays your money and takes your choice. Treat yourself to an organic bird and be reminded of how chicken used to taste and why it was saved for high days and holidays.

After-work coq au vin

Serves 4   *25 minutes preparation: 45 minutes cooking*

I hesitate to claim this as an authentic coq au vin, but this close approximation is made with conveniently prepared chicken pieces. My choice would be free-range legs, which are easily jointed before cooking, but you may find thighs more convenient. Either way, I think the dish is preferable if the chicken is skinned, because even though the pieces are floured and browned before they are cooked with wine and seasonings, the skin always ends up flabby. Also, in this relatively quick version, there is only time to marinate the chicken for about 15 minutes, so minus skin and with a few nicks in the meat, the marinade is more likely to impart its flavor.

4 whole chicken legs or 8 large thighs
1 bay leaf
2 glasses red wine, about 1¼ cups
2 sprigs thyme
1 small sprig rosemary
3oz/85g pancetta cubes or chopped lean bacon
½ stick butter
2 onions
4 garlic cloves

10oz/300g medium-size mushrooms
4 tbsp all-purpose flour
1 tbsp vegetable oil
½ chicken stock cube dissolved in 1¼ cups
  boiling water
1lb/500g small new potatoes, boiled and peeled
2 cups baby peas (optional)
1 tbsp chopped parsley
salt and freshly ground black pepper

If preferred, skin the pieces of chicken. Halve the legs, if using, at the joint. Make small incisions in the chicken in several places. Put the pieces in a bowl with the bay leaf, red wine, thyme, and rosemary. Let marinate while you prepare everything else. Put the pancetta in a large, heavy-bottom pan over low heat and cook very slowly with half the butter, increasing the heat slightly after 5 minutes. While cooking, peel and halve the onions, then finely slice into half moons. Peel and coarsely chop the garlic. Add the onions to the pan and season with salt and pepper, then cover and cook for 10 minutes, or until tender. Add the garlic and cook for one minute.

Meanwhile, wipe and slice the mushrooms. Stir them into the onions, adjusting the heat so the mushrooms begin to soften. Season again, cook for a couple more minutes, then scoop the onion mixture onto a plate. Remove the chicken pieces from the marinade, shaking them dry. Season thoroughly, then sift the flour over the chicken pieces so they are thoroughly dusted. Add the remaining butter and cooking oil to the pan, then return it to medium heat and brown the pieces of chicken. Add the marinade, then turn up the heat and bring to a boil, stirring constantly as you do so in order that the browned flour on the chicken thickens the sauce. Cook for a couple of minutes, then add the stock and stir as the sauce comes back to a boil.

Return the onion and pancetta mixture to the pan and simmer gently for about 20 minutes, or until the chicken is cooked. Taste and adjust the seasoning. Add the cooked potatoes 5 minutes before serving to warm them and, if using, the peas. Garnish with chopped parsley.

Cheat's chicken-and-leek risotto with saffron

Serves 2–3 *20 minutes preparation: 40 minutes cooking*

Most people love risotto but hate the thought of standing over a hot stove for the best part of a half-hour stirring ladle after ladle of hot stock into the rice. This simple variation on the risotto theme virtually cooks itself and is mindless to make. It isn't made with a risotto rice such as arborio, vialone nano, or Spanish carnaroli. Good old basmati makes a terrific risotto-type slop and if the dish is left around to go cold, it becomes the most fabulous filling for a puff-pastry pie. The recipe could also be turned into a soupy meal-in-a-bowl by stirring a dessertspoon of all-purpose flour into the cooked chicken and dissolving a chicken stock cube in 4 cups water.

1 onion	2 skinless boned chicken thighs
1 garlic clove	1 small unwaxed lemon
¼ stick butter	generous pinch saffron dissolved in 1 tbsp hot water
1 tbsp olive oil	¾ cup basmati rice
1 bay leaf	2 tbsp chopped flatleaf parsley
2 leeks	salt and freshly ground black pepper

Peel and halve the onion and garlic, then finely chop. Melt the butter with the olive oil in an 8-cup-capacity heavy-bottom pan with a well-fitting lid. Stir in the onion, garlic, and bay leaf. Cook, stirring often, for 5 minutes while you trim the leeks and slice into thin circles. Wash the leeks and shake dry. Stir the leeks into the onion and season generously with salt and pepper. Stir again, then cover the pan and cook for 5 minutes, stirring once or twice.

Meanwhile, slice the chicken into bite-size strips. Season the pieces with salt and pepper. Remove the zest from half the lemon, either with a zester or using a potato peeler, cutting small, paper-thin scraps. Stir the chicken, lemon zest, and saffron into the vegetables and cook, uncovered, stirring to ensure all the chicken turns from pink to white, for 5 minutes.

Rinse the rice, then shake dry and stir it into the pan. Add 1½ cups water and the juice from half the lemon, then bring the liquid to a boil. Reduce the heat immediately to very low, then cover the pan and cook for 10 minutes. Remove and let the pan stand untouched for an additional 10 minutes so the rice finishes cooking in the steam. Stir the parsley into the risotto and adjust the seasoning with salt, pepper, and lemon juice, then serve, risotto-style, in bowls.

Chicken with lemon couscous and black olives

Serves 4   *20 minutes preparation: 15 minutes cooking*

These days, if you want to cut a dash with a quick impromptu supper for friends, the smart ingredient to reach for is couscous. Pasta, useful and delicious though it undoubtedly is, seems passé by comparison. I know, I know, it is ridiculous to compare these two ancient foods, but let me explain that this particular version of couscous was whipped up under testing circumstances. I was visiting a friend who lives part of the year in an isolated cottage. He has no running water and cooks with a single burner that has about as much power as a fading blow torch. Despite the obvious handicaps for this metropolitan cook, the dish was a huge hit, as much for its originality as for the ease with which it was made. It goes spectacularly well with chunks of cucumber in plain yogurt beaten with crushed garlic, a splash of lemon juice, and olive oil.

1oz/25g golden raisins
4 large chicken breast fillets
2 lemons (1 for juice, 1 for wedges)
4 tbsp olive oil
2 garlic cloves
1oz/25g pine nuts
pinch saffron

1 chicken stock cube dissolved in 1³/₄ cups
   boiling water
7oz/200g couscous
1oz/25g pitted black olives
few sprigs cilantro
salt

Place the golden raisins in a cup and just cover with boiling water. Let stand to plump. Slice the chicken into 2in/5cm strips, approximately ½ in/1cm thick. Put the chicken in a shallow dish and squeeze over the juice from half a lemon. Add 1 tablespoon of the olive oil. Peel the garlic and chop finely, then sprinkle with a little salt and crush to a paste. Add the paste to the bowl and mix everything thoroughly. Leave for at least 10 minutes and up to 2 hours.

Heat ½ tablespoon of the olive oil in a skillet placed over medium heat and stir-fry the pine nuts for a couple of minutes until lightly golden. Tip onto absorbent paper towels to drain. Stir the saffron into the chicken stock. Pour the couscous into a bowl, then stir in the stock, the juice from the remaining lemon half, and 1 tablespoon of the olive oil. Season with salt and pepper and stir, then cover and let stand for the couscous to hydrate. Check after 10 minutes: it should be slightly more moist than the usual bone dry. Fork up the couscous, then stir in the golden raisins and pine nuts and spoon onto a platter. Tear the olives in half and scatter over the top.

Add the last of the oil to the skillet placed over high heat. Cook the chicken in batches to encourage fast, even cooking. Allow about 30 seconds a side until golden. Arrange the chicken over the couscous as each batch is ready. Decorate with sprigs of cilantro and lemon wedges. Eat hot, warm, or cold.

Chicken pilaf

Serves 4   *20 minutes preparation: 40 minutes cooking*

Here's a fantastic way of using the remains of a roast chicken or a small amount of cooked chicken to feed four. Modest ingredients are enlivened with a hint of cinnamon and saffron to become an unbelievably luscious and extremely more-ish dish. For a change, you could also serve the pilaf on a platter garnished with a couple of sliced, hard-boiled eggs to create a beautiful Indian-style biryani. If you have all the necessary ingredients to hand except saffron, the pilaf will still be delicious. A generous pinch of turmeric will color the rice similarly, but you will miss out on the beguiling saffron flavor and aroma.

2 large onions
1 tbsp olive oil
⅓ cup blanched almonds
½ stick butter
1 chicken stock cube
generous 1 cup basmati rice
9oz/250g cooked chicken

handful broken vermicelli or fine thread
  egg noodles
⅓ cup raisins
½ tsp ground cinnamon
generous pinch saffron
salt and freshly ground black pepper
1 lemon, cut into wedges

Peel and halve the onions. Keeping separate piles, thinly slice one half and finely chop the rest. Heat the olive oil in a medium-size pan and, when very hot, stir in the sliced onion. Adjust the heat so the onion sizzles without burning and cook for several minutes until nicely browned and shriveled. Add the almonds and cook for another minute or so until they take on a bit of color. Tip the mixture onto absorbent paper towels to drain. Wipe out the pan and add the butter. As soon as it is melted, stir in the chopped onion and cook for about 15 minutes, stirring often, until soft and golden.

Meanwhile, prepare everything else. Wash the rice until the water runs clear. Dissolve the stock cube in scant 3 cups boiling water. Tear the chicken into bite-size pieces and season generously with salt and pepper. When the onions are ready, stir the vermicelli into the onions and cook for a couple of minutes until golden. Now add the raisins and cook for an additional minute or two before adding the cinnamon and rice. Dissolve the saffron in 2 tablespoons water and add that too. Stir well and cook for 2 more minutes before adding the hot stock. Bring the liquid to a boil, then reduce the heat to very low and cook, covered, for 10 minutes.

Turn off the heat and let stand without removing the lid for an additional 10 minutes. Stir the chicken into the pilaf and pile into a serving bowl. Garnish with the browned onion and almonds. Serve with lemon wedges to squeeze over the rice. The pilaf is delicious hot, warm, or cold, although it does turn stodgy as it cools.

Chicken with cilantro and tomatoes

Serves 4   *35 minutes preparation: 35 minutes cooking*

A hint of tamarind complements the lemony tang of cilantro in this wonderfully rustic chicken and tomato stew. It is easy to make and everybody always seems to like it. The pieces of chicken end up imbued with a fresh tomato sauce, which is thickened with red onions and freshened up with the last-minute addition of masses of chopped cilantro leaves, garlic, and a little mint. This dish was inspired by something similar I once ate in Portugal. It goes with just about everything, from boiled potatoes, to pasta, rice, or a chunk of bread.

1lb 10oz/750g skinned lean chicken pieces
3 tbsp olive oil
3 red onions
large knob butter
1lb 10oz/750g ripe tomatoes
1 bay leaf

1 tbsp tamarind paste
3 garlic cloves, preferably new season
1 large bunch cilantro, about 3oz/85g
1 small bunch mint, about 2oz/55g
salt and freshly ground black pepper

Slice the chicken into thick strips, cutting across the grain. Heat 2 tablespoons of the oil in a pan that can accommodate all the ingredients. When the oil is very hot, cook the pieces of chicken in batches, cooking for a couple of minutes a side without moving, then turning as the chicken browns and turns crusty. Remove the chicken from the pan.

Meanwhile, peel and halve the onions and slice down the halves to make chunky wedges. When the chicken is all done, add the butter and, as soon as it has sizzled, stir in the onions. Cook briskly, stirring every now and again, until the onions are wilted and scorched in places. While the onions are cooking, place the tomatoes in a bowl and cover with boiling water. Count to 20, then drain, peel and chop. Stir the tamarind, bay leaf, and tomatoes into the onions. Cook for 10–15 minutes, or until the tomatoes have broken down a bit, then return the chicken to the pan.

Cook at a steady simmer for about 20 minutes, or until the chicken is tender. Taste and adjust the seasoning with salt and pepper. Peel the garlic and chop very finely. Coarsely chop the leaves from the bunches of cilantro and mint. When the chicken is done and the tomatoes and onions have made a thick, chunky sauce, stir in the chopped herbs and the finely chopped garlic and serve.

Chicken with lentils and bacon

Serves 4–5   *20 minutes preparation: 25 minutes cooking*

A comforting, stewy dish that takes no time to cook and instantly fills the kitchen with delicious homely smells. Most ingredients are fresh and their choice and the way they are prepared are crucial to the speed of the dish. Leftovers reheat perfectly.

2 red onions
2 large garlic cloves
¼ stick butter
1 tbsp cooking oil
2 celery stalks
2 carrots
1 bay leaf
1lb/450g skinless boned chicken

½ tsp thyme leaves
6 medium tomatoes, about 1lb/500g
14oz/400g canned green lentils
squeeze lemon juice
3½oz/100g bacon
1 cup frozen peas
1 tbsp coarsely chopped flatleaf parsley
salt and freshly ground black pepper

Peel and halve the onions, then slice. Peel and coarsely chop the garlic. Melt half the butter with half the cooking oil in a spacious pan over medium heat. Add the onion and garlic, then season generously with salt and pepper and cook until the onion is wilted and juicy.

Meanwhile, trim the celery and carrots and peel both with a potato peeler. Finely slice the celery and grate the carrots. Add both, and the bay leaf, to the onion and season again with salt and pepper, then cook, stirring a few times, for 5 minutes. While the vegetable are cooking, slice the chicken across the grain into 1½ x ½in/3.5 x 1cm strips. Sprinkle it with the thyme.

Place the tomatoes in a bowl and cover with boiling water. Count to 20, then drain and use a small knife to cut the cores out in a cone shape and remove the skin. Tip the lentils into a strainer and rinse with cold water. Shake dry.

Add the chicken to the vegetables with the remaining butter and oil, and stir around as the chicken plumps and turns white all over. Now add the tomatoes, crushing them down into the pan to break them up. Squeeze over the lemon juice and continue cooking until the tomatoes have flopped to make a juicy sauce. This takes 10–15 minutes. While it is cooking, slice across the bacon strips to make little sticks. Heat a small skillet and cook the bacon until it is very crisp. Tip onto absorbent paper towels to drain.

When the sauce is ready, add the prepared lentils and frozen peas. Simmer for a couple of minutes to heat the lentils, then taste and adjust the seasoning with salt and pepper. Serve with a garnish of parsley and crisp bacon bits.

Chicken and cashew nut noodle stir-fry

Serves 2   *15 minutes preparation: 10 minutes cooking*

The shops are awash with stir-fry sauces and every condiment needed for authentic and ersatz Chinese food, but this simple stir-fry requires nothing more than soy sauce and sherry to give the dish a recognizable Chinese flavor. Marinating the chicken in a mixture of egg white, cornstarch, and salt has the double effect of softening the texture of the meat and providing a thin, light batter. As always with stir-fries, the important point is to get all the slicing done before you start cooking and to line up the ingredients so they are quick and easy to fling into the wok. Rice noodles have become familiar through Thai cooking and the ones you want have various names but look like thin, off-white tagliatelle and are folded like a skein of wool before they are stuffed into their cellophane packages. They don't need to be cooked and just require a few minutes soaking in boiling water before they turn snowy white. The quantities given provide plenty for two greedy portions, but leftovers are delicious cold—perfect, I'd say, for tomorrow's lunch box.

2 chicken breast fillets	**2 tbsp soy sauce (I use Kikkoman)**
1 egg white	**2 tbsp dry sherry**
2 tsp cornstarch	**small bunch chives (optional)**
3oz/85g flat rice noodles	**3 tbsp vegetable oil**
1oz/25g piece fresh gingerroot	**⅓ cup cashew nuts**
4oz/125g bunch scallions	**salt**

Slice the chicken into thin, bite-size strips. Whisk the egg white with the cornstarch and ½ teaspoon salt until fluffy, white, and smooth. Immerse the chicken in the mixture and chill in the refrigerator while you prepare everything else. Place the noodles in a pan or bowl and cover with boiling water. Cover and let stand for at least 4 minutes to soften. Drain them just before you begin to cook.

Peel the ginger and slice into short, thin sticks. Trim the scallions and slice into skinny strips the length of your little finger. Measure out the soy and sherry. Snip the chives, if using.

Heat the wok over a high flame. Add 2 tablespoons of the oil and swirl it round the wok. Add the chicken and quickly spread it out, turning it almost immediately and adjusting the heat so it forms a thin crust that doesn't blacken. Once all the meat has turned white and is patched with golden brown—after about 1 minute—tip it onto a plate.

Wipe out the wok, then add the rest of the oil and stir-fry the cashew nuts, ginger, and scallions for a minute or so until the onions wilt. Add the soy mixture and return the chicken. Stir-fry for another 30 seconds, then add the noodles and mix. Remove from the heat, then stir in the chives, if using, and tip into bowls. Eat with chopsticks or a fork.

Chicken tom yam

Serves 4   *20 minutes preparation: 30 minutes cooking*

This is a great soup if you're feeling a bit jaded. One whiff clears the sinuses and brings tears to the eyes. Its golden broth is an unholy balance of hot and sour from chiles, lime juice, and salty Thai fish sauce with a complementary undercurrent of lemongrass and ginger. This addictive liquid is good enough to drink as a tonic, although it is quickly turned into a delicious healthy, lowfat soup with even more layers of flavor. It's most often made with shrimp (tom yam kung), occasionally with white fish or squid, and is sometimes on restaurant menus as a vegetarian option with tofu and mushrooms. My meal-in-a-bowl version is a slightly more elaborate mixture of flavors and textures than is usual. Although this soup is at its most superior when made with fresh chicken stock, it's still worth making with stock cubes.

3 lemongrass stems
1oz/25g piece fresh gingerroot
4 small green chiles
6¼ cups chicken stock
4 large chicken thighs
5oz/150g white mushrooms

generous ⅓ cup green beans
4 scallions
1 tbsp cilantro leaves
3 limes (2 for juice, 1 for wedges)
2 tbsp Thai fish sauce (*nam pla*)
salt

Smash the lemongrass stems with something heavy to split them. Peel and finely slice the ginger, cutting it into short, thin sticks. Place the lemongrass, ginger, chiles, and ½ teaspoon salt in a pan with the stock. Bring to a boil, then reduce the heat and simmer, covered, for 15 minutes.

Meanwhile, skin the chicken and cut off the bone into bite-size chunks. Wipe, then halve the mushrooms or cut into fourths. Trim the beans and slice into small pieces. Finely slice the scallions. Coarsely chop the cilantro. Fish the lemongrass out of the stock and, if you are a chile freak, finely slice the chiles and return. If not, remove them.

Stir the juice from 2 of the limes and the fish sauce into the pot, then add chicken and mushrooms. Cook gently for 10 minutes without boiling. Add the beans and scallions. Cook for an additional couple of minutes, then stir in the cilantro leaves and serve with a wedge of lime.

Chicken and shrimp gumbo

Serves 4   *20 minutes preparation: 30 minutes cooking*

In Louisiana, the dish everyone loves and has a view about is gumbo. Some people guard their family recipes as if they were the key to heaven, but this hearty Creole or Cajun meal-in-a-bowl is always hot enough to remind you that this is Tabasco country. My quick, after-work version doesn't fall into the usual gumbo categories in that it isn't thickened with okra or filé, a powder made from dried young sassafras leaves, which originally came from the Choctaw Indians. Gumbo always includes the famous Creole trinity of celery, onion, and green bell pepper and this one is colored as well as thickened with paprika. Any mild paprika would be fine, but I recommend "soft" smoked paprika if you can find it. Serve as a soup or spoon it over boiled rice.

1 large celery heart	½ tsp thyme
1 green bell pepper	1 chicken stock cube
1 onion	1 tsp "soft" smoked paprika
2 garlic cloves	½ tbsp all-purpose flour
1 leek	3 tsp Tabasco sauce
2 fresh or canned peeled tomatoes	generous handful flatleaf parsley leaves
4 large chicken thighs	about 9oz/250g cooked shelled shrimp
4 tbsp cooking oil	squeeze lemon or lime juice
1 bay leaf	salt

Finely slice the celery. Wash and shake dry. Dice the bell pepper, discarding the seeds and white membrane. Peel and halve the onion, then finely chop. Peel and thinly slice the garlic. Trim and split the leek and slice thinly. Chop the tomatoes. Remove the skin from the chicken and slice the meat off the bone into bite-size chunks.

Heat 1 tablespoon of the oil in a spacious heavy-bottom pan and quickly brown the chicken in batches, transferring it to a plate as you go. Heat the remaining oil in the pan and stir in the onion, pepper, celery, garlic, bay leaf, and thyme. Cook briskly, stirring often, for about 10 minutes, or until the vegetables are juicy and beginning to soften but not brown. Add the leek and cook for a couple of minutes.

Dissolve the stock cube in 2½ cups hot water. Sprinkle the paprika and flour over the vegetables, then stir well and cook for a minute before adding the chicken, stock, and Tabasco. Bring to a boil, then immediately turn down the heat and simmer for 10 minutes.

Meanwhile, coarsely chop the parsley. Add the parsley, shrimp, and tomato to the pan. Reheat, then taste and adjust the seasoning with salt and lemon juice. Serve immediately or reheat as required, adding extra parsley for color.

Chinese noodle salad

Serves 3–4 *20 minutes preparation: 20 minutes cooking*

Cucumber is the novelty in this delicious dish, inspired by something I once ate at Mr Kai in Mayfair, London. The cucumber strips soften slightly in the noodle heat, but the joy of this dish is the contrast of textures as well as the subtle flavors. It's the perfect refrigerator standby and ideal for lunch boxes because it's a complete meal that is satisfying and relatively healthy.

½ chicken stock cube
1oz/25g piece fresh gingerroot, sliced
2–4 garlic cloves, crushed (optional)
4 scallions
4 large chicken thighs or 2 legs
1 red chile

½ cucumber
5oz/150g fine thread egg noodles
1 tbsp cider vinegar
1 tbsp toasted sesame oil
squeeze lemon juice
salt

Place the stock cube, 2½ cups water, most of the sliced ginger, the crushed garlic cloves, and scallion greens in a medium-size pan. Season lightly with salt and bring to a boil. Trim away any excess fat and skin from the chicken thighs or, if using legs, joint them with a sharp knife. Add the chicken to the boiling stock, then return the liquid to a boil and immediately turn the heat to low. Cover the pan and simmer for 15 minutes.

Meanwhile, finely slice the white of the scallions. Split the chile and scrape away the seeds. Slice into skinny batons and then into tiny dice. Cut the remaining ginger into tiny dice. Split the cucumber in half lengthwise. Use a teaspoon to scrape out the seeds and their watery surrounds. Halve the cucumber across the width. Slice each half lengthwise into very thin ribbons, each with a share of dark green skin.

Check that the chicken is cooked through and lift out of the pan onto a cutting board. Scoop the ginger slices and scallion greens out of the pan (leave the garlic) and add the noodles. Increase the heat to boil the stock, tossing the noodles to disentangle and keep submerged. Reduce the heat slightly and boil gently for 3 minutes, or until most of the stock has been absorbed. Cover the pan and turn off the heat, but keep covered for a minute or so until the stock is completely absorbed, leaving the noodles glossy.

Tip the noodles into a serving bowl. Add the vinegar and sesame oil and toss thoroughly. Discard the chicken skin and use a fork and sharp knife to shred the chicken meat. Add it and all the other ingredients and toss well. Season with lemon juice, then toss again and serve.

Cock-a-leekie

Serves 2–3   *15 minutes preparation: 40 minutes cooking*

This adaptation of the famous Scottish soup makes a wonderful, comforting supper. Not only does the dish look interesting—black prunes against white chicken and verdant leek greens—but it is also a surprisingly good mix of textures and flavors. It is particularly delicious with brown bread and butter and a nip of whisky.

4 skinless chicken thighs
large bunch flatleaf parsley, about 3oz/85g
1 bay leaf
3 sprigs thyme
2 garlic cloves

3 medium leeks, about 6oz/175g
1 small onion
10 prunes
½ cup basmati rice
salt and freshly ground black pepper

Place the chicken thighs in a medium-size pan with scant 3 cups water. Bring slowly to a boil. Remove the gray scum that forms. Meanwhile, pick the leaves off the parsley and set aside. Bundle the parsley stems, bay leaf, and thyme together with cotton or string. Crush the garlic cloves and flake away the skin. Trim the leeks and slice the white part into 1in/2.5cm circles. Peel and halve the onion, then thinly slice. Add the herb bundle, garlic, leeks, and onion to the pan. Add ½ teaspoon salt and plenty of black pepper. Return to a boil, then reduce the heat and simmer gently for 15 minutes.

Meanwhile, finely slice the leek greens, discarding only the very fibrous ends. Rinse and shake dry. If necessary, remove the pits from the prunes. Coarsely chop the parsley leaves: you want about 3 tablespoons. Discard the herb bundle and add the rice to the pan, letting it trickle under the leeks (which will float on top). Return to a boil, then reduce the heat immediately and simmer for 15 minutes. Five minutes before the end of cooking add the prunes, poking them among the now plump rice. Add the leek greens and half the parsley. Simmer briskly for 3 minutes—the leek greens should remain *al dente*.

Let rest for a couple of minutes, then stir in the remaining parsley. Taste and adjust the seasoning. For ease of eating, and to make the chicken go farther, cut the meat off the bones before you serve. This is best done before the leek greens are added.

Corn and broiled red bell pepper chicken chowder

Serves 4   *25 minutes preparation: 35 minutes cooking*

The time to make this soup is toward the end of the summer, when corn-on-the-cob and sweet red bell peppers are so cheap they're almost being given away. The crunch of the corn goes well with the soft chunks of chicken, the slippery pieces of broiled red bell pepper, and strands of onion. Everything is livened up with the occasional sting of chile and curious charm of cilantro. Broiling the bell peppers, incidentally, does not just make them easy to peel: Like roasting, it concentrates their flavor and means they will be almost cooked when they join the other ingredients in the pan.

2 red bell peppers
1 red onion
¼ stick butter
1 tbsp cooking oil
1 plump garlic clove
1 small red chile

2 corn-on-the-cob
1lb/500g boneless chicken
large bunch cilantro, about 3oz/85g
1 chicken stock cube dissolved in generous
   2 cups boiling water
salt and freshly ground black pepper

Pre-heat the overhead broiler to its highest setting. Lay the red bell peppers out on the broiler pan. Place it close to the hot broiler and cook the bell peppers, turning every few minutes, until their skin is blistered and blackened all over. Place the bell peppers in a sealed plastic bag or in a bowl covered with plastic wrap. Leave for about 10 minutes to sweat and "lift" the skin. Peel away the charred skin. Cut the bell peppers into fourths lengthwise and discard the stem, white seeds, and membrane, then chop into pieces the size of a postage stamp.

Meanwhile, peel and halve the onion, then finely slice into half moons. Place a pan that can hold the entire dish over medium heat. Add the butter and cooking oil and, when the butter has melted, stir in the onion. Let it soften without coloring, allowing at least 10 minutes, probably 15. While the onion is cooking, peel and finely chop the garlic. Split the chile and use a teaspoon to scrape away the seeds, then chop very finely. Remove the cob leaves and "silk" if necessary. Trim the end of the cob, then stand upright and use a large, sharp knife to slice the kernels off the cob. Discard the cob.

Slice the chicken into kabob-size chunks. Coarsely chop the bunch of cilantro, stems included, setting aside 2 tablespoons of leaves. When the onion is ready, stir in the garlic and chile. Cook until the garlic is aromatic—not long—then stir in the corn kernels. Cover the pan, then reduce the heat slightly and cook, stirring a couple of times, for 10 minutes.

Add the chicken, tossing it around until it is all white. Add most of the cilantro and the diced red bell pepper. Season generously with salt and pepper. Add the stock. Bring to a boil, then reduce the heat immediately and simmer for 5–10 minutes, or until the chicken is tender. Taste and adjust the seasoning with salt and pepper. Add the remaining cilantro, then stir and serve.

Japanese chicken in a bowl with ponzu

Serves 4   *20 minutes preparation: 15 minutes cooking*

If you can imagine minestrone with a pungent sour sauce instead of the pesto-style sharpener that lifts this chunky soup, then you are well on the way to understanding this dish. It is the mix of textures as well as flavors that makes this meal-in-a-bowl. If you are lucky enough to have some homemade stock, now is the time to use it. The great thing about the dish is that the chicken and vegetables contribute to the flavor of the broth as they cook. Although I have made this with chicken, it could be made with a firm-textured fish such as angler fish or hoki, or with tofu if you are a vegetarian. The soup is delicious enough on its own but the salty, citrus ponzu *liquor gives it an incredible lift. Any rice noodles or just-soak Japanese noodles such as soba or medium egg noodles, are perfect for this dish. I used the ones that look like tagliatelle and their softness added bulk without interfering with texture or flavor. Mirin, a sweet, distilled rice wine, and rice vinegar are available in most supermarkets and health stores.*

5oz/150g rice noodles
4 cups chicken stock or 2 stock cubes
   dissolved in 4 cups hot water
4 large chicken thighs
1 carrot, about 3½oz/100g
4oz/125g shiitake mushrooms
1 leek
½ cucumber

1¼ cups snow peas or sugar snap peas
3½oz/100g spinach
3 tbsp mirin
1 lemon
1 lime
3 tbsp dark soy sauce
3 tbsp rice vinegar

Generously cover the noodles with boiling water, then cover and let soften. Bring the stock to a boil in a large pan. Cut the chicken into bite-size chunks and add to the stock. Return to boiling, then adjust the heat so the liquid simmers. Cook the chicken for 6 minutes.

Meanwhile, keeping everything in separate piles, peel and slice the carrot. Wipe and slice the mushrooms. Trim the leek and slice in thin circles. Peel the cucumber, then halve it lengthwise and use a teaspoon to scrape out the seeds and watery surround, then slice in chunky half moons. Halve the snow peas lengthwise. Shred the spinach.

Add the carrot to the chicken. Cook for 2 minutes, then add the mushrooms. Cook for an additional 2 minutes and add the leek. Now add the cucumber and, 2 minutes later, the snow peas. Drain the noodles and add them. Stir in the spinach and turn off the heat.

Make the *ponzu* by pouring the mirin into a small pan. Quickly bring to a boil and boil for 10 seconds. Pour it into a bowl, then add the juice from the lemon and lime, the soy sauce, and vinegar. Mix thoroughly. Serve the soup with chopsticks and a spoon and a bowl of *ponzu* for dunking the big chunks and seasoning the soup.

Magenta chicken curry

Serves 4   *20 minutes preparation: 55 minutes cooking*

Now that beet has been claimed as a health food which can do wonders for your love-life, I've been trying out a few alternatives to the British salad staple of beet in vinegar. When grated and boiled in water, it produces the most exquisitely vibrant purple liquid, which has the power to turn pale food into magenta-colored masterpieces. It brings a new vivacity to curries and is a new take on your average "ruby" (Cockney rhyming slang for a curry). This chicken curry looks spectacular served with a scoop of white yogurt, and has a deliciously intriguing flavor that is all at once hot, sweet, and sour. Serve it in a warmed tortilla with yogurt and a few sprigs of cilantro or over rice with yogurt or raita, mango chutney, and poppadoms.

1 dried red chile
1 onion
3 tbsp vegetable oil
3 plump garlic cloves
2oz/55g piece fresh gingerroot
1lb 10oz/750g boneless chicken

1 tbsp ground coriander
7oz/200g strained plain yogurt
2 raw beet
1 small lemon
salt

Place the chile in a cup and just cover with boiling water. Let soak while you peel and finely chop the onion. Heat the oil in a large skillet or similarly wide-based pan placed over medium-low heat. Add the onion and cook, stirring occasionally, for 6–7 minutes, or until soft and golden.

Meanwhile, peel and finely chop the garlic. Peel the ginger and slice thinly into small scraps. Cut the chicken into bite-size pieces. Remove the chile from its soaking water. Split it lengthwise, then scrape away the seeds and chop into tiny pieces. Stir the garlic, ginger, and chile into the softened onion and cook for an additional 3–4 minutes. Add the ground coriander and cook for an additional 30 seconds. Increase the heat slightly, then add the chicken to the skillet and stir-fry for 5–6 minutes, or until all the pieces have turned from pink to white. Season the chicken with ½ teaspoon salt and stir in the yogurt. Reduce the heat to low, then cover the pan—use a double fold of foil if your skillet doesn't have a lid—and cook for 15 minutes.

Meanwhile, use a potato peeler to peel the beet and grate them on the large hole of a cheese grater directly into a small pan. Add 1¼ cups water and the juice of half the lemon and cook, partially covered, for 10–15 minutes, or until the beet is tender. Tip the beet and water into the chicken. Stir thoroughly and cook, uncovered, for an additional 5–10 minutes, or until the curry is thick and all the flavors amalgamated. Taste and adjust the seasoning with salt and lemon juice. This curry reheats perfectly.

Quick cassoulet

Serves 4   *30 minutes preparation: 60 minutes cooking*

It was talk of what to do with the remains of the Christmas goose that started me off. In the Languedoc, where cassoulet originates, it's a complex, hearty concoction of preserved duck, lamb, pork, sausages, and dried lima beans. The stew simmers away for hours and is ready when the meat is meltingly soft and the beans have soaked up all the stock. A crusty topping of bread crumbs and parsley absorbs any fat and keeps the dish moist. This relatively quick version is made along the same lines. It's extremely tasty and satisfying. Serve with lemon wedges to squeeze over the top and lightly cooked green beans.

1 large onion
3 large garlic cloves
2 tbsp cooking oil
4 strips rindless lean bacon
1 bay leaf
½ tsp thyme
1 tsp chopped sage
4 good-quality pork sausages
14oz/400g canned peeled tomatoes

½ chicken stock cube dissolved in 1¼ cups
   hot water
4 skinless duck breasts
14oz/400g canned cannellini or similar white beans
2 tbsp chopped flatleaf parsley
2oz/65g stale bread, without crusts
1–2 tbsp olive oil
salt and freshly ground black pepper

Peel and halve the onion, then finely slice. Peel and slice 2 of the garlic cloves. Heat 1 tablespoon of the cooking oil in a large, heavy-bottom pan until very hot. Stir in the onion. Cook, stirring often, for 4 minutes. Salt generously, then reduce the heat to low. Stir in the sliced garlic, then cover the pan and let cook for 10 minutes.

Slice the bacon across the strips and add to the pan with the bay leaf, thyme, and sage. Increase the heat slightly and quickly brown the sausages. Add the tomatoes, breaking them up in the pan, and the stock. Season lightly with salt and generously with black pepper. Simmer, uncovered, for 15 minutes, so the sausages poach and the liquid thickens and reduces.

Meanwhile, cut each duck breast into four large pieces. Heat the remaining cooking oil in a skillet and brown the duck. Add the duck and its juices to the pan. Rinse the beans and add them too. Establish a gentle simmer. Stir in 1 tablespoon of the parsley and check the seasoning, adjusting as necessary. Blitz the bread and the remaining garlic clove to make crumbs, and stir in the remaining parsley. Spread the breadcrumb mixture over the top of the cassoulet, then cover the pan and cook for 30 minutes.

Pre-heat the overhead broiler. Remove the pan lid, then criss-cross the cassoulet with a thin stream of olive oil and place the pan under the broiler. Cook until crusty and golden, but watch like a hawk to avoid burning.

Borscht with chicken

Serves 4   *30 minutes preparation: 50 minutes cooking*

There's no such thing as a definitive recipe for borscht, the famous sweet-sour beet soup from the Ukraine. There are many regional variations made with different vegetables apart from the ubiquitous beet, some with meat and others with mushrooms. I've even come across a fish version with cucumber instead of the more usual cabbage, carrot, and potato. One of the finest recipes requires discarding the vegetables after they've flavored and clarified the broth to reveal a sparklingly clear magenta soup. In this borscht, the soup is thick with vegetables and the broth is flavored in the traditional way with beer—if it is flat, so much the better. I've added two chicken legs to enrich the flavors and turn the soup into more of a meal. If you don't eat meat, leave out the chicken and the stock cube which, I think, give the soup a bit more oomph.

1 large onion
2 large garlic cloves
2 tbsp olive oil
1 large raw beet, about 11½oz/325g, and 1 small
    raw beet, about 5oz/150g
13oz/375g waxy potatoes
2 medium carrots
2 free-range chicken legs or 4 large thighs or
    drumsticks

1¼ cups beer
½ chicken stock cube
9oz/250g red cabbage
7oz/200g canned chopped tomatoes
2 tbsp balsamic or other good red wine vinegar
1–2 tsp sugar
sour cream
dill or chives
salt and freshly ground black pepper

Peel, then halve and finely slice the onion. Peel the garlic and slice very thinly. Heat the oil in a large pan and stir both in. Add salt and cook for 10 minutes, or until floppy and golden.

Meanwhile, peel the large beet and chop into small dice. Do the same with the potato and carrots. Stir the diced beet and potatoes into the onion and cook for a couple of minutes, then add the carrots and chicken. Pour on the beer and 4 cups cold water and crumble in the stock cube. Bring the soup to a boil—this takes several minutes—and adjust the heat so it simmers steadily when three-quarters covered with a lid. Cook for 15 minutes.

Meanwhile, cut the cabbage into fourths and core, then slice as thinly as possible. Add to the soup with the tomatoes, vinegar, and a generous pinch of salt. Stir well, then increase the heat and return to a boil. Adjust the heat again as before, then cover as before and cook for an additional 15 minutes, or until all the vegetables are tender. Taste the broth and adjust and balance the seasoning with salt, pepper, sugar, and possibly a dash more vinegar. Peel the small beet and grate it directly into the soup to inject deep color and fresh flavor. Cook for an additional 5–10 minutes.

Remove the chicken and flake the meat off the bones into the soup (or garnish individual servings). Serve the soup immediately or, better still, let sit, covered, for up to 30 minutes before serving with a blob of sour cream and a final garnish of snipped herbs.

Moroccan chicken, egg, and almond tagine

Serves 2 *20 minutes preparation: 35 minutes cooking*

The tagines of Morocco are perfect dishes to serve at any time of the year, whatever the weather. This one is a new, after-work favorite and transforms chicken fillets into something really interesting and satisfying. If you want to make the dish for four people, just double up on the ingredients. If you don't like garlic—though the resultant flavor is very subtle, contributing to the overall interest of the dish—then leave it out. The perfect accompaniment is couscous. For two generous portions, you will need 3½oz/100g couscous hydrated in 1 cup boiling water. A splash of olive oil or a knob of butter with a squeeze of lemon makes it more interesting.

2 large onions, about 10oz/300g in total
3 tbsp olive oil
¼ stick butter
½ tsp ground cumin
½ tsp ground coriander
generous pinch saffron
2 boneless chicken breasts

1 large garlic clove
2 eggs, hard-cooked
½ tbsp vegetable oil
scant ¼ cup blanched almonds
large bunch cilantro
1 lemon or lime (for wedges)
salt and freshly ground black pepper

Peel and halve the onions. Slice one very thinly and finely chop the other. Heat 2 tablespoons of the olive oil and the butter in an 8-cup-capacity, heavy-bottom pan placed over medium heat. When the butter has melted, stir in the onions. Cook for 5 minutes, then stir in the cumin and ground coriander and a generous seasoning of salt and pepper. Soften the saffron in 1 tablespoon boiling water and add that too. Reduce the heat, then cover the pan and cook for 15 minutes.

Meanwhile, slice the chicken into bite-size strips. Peel and finely chop the garlic. Sprinkle it with ½ teaspoon salt and use a pestle and mortar or the flat of a knife to work to a juicy paste. Stir the remaining olive oil into the garlic and smear it all over the chicken. Peel the eggs and cut into fourths. Heat the vegetable oil in a second skillet and stir-fry the almonds for a couple of minutes until evenly golden. Tip onto absorbent paper towels to drain.

When the onions are ready, stir in the chicken and cook, stirring frequently, for a couple of minutes until all the pieces have turned white. Add just enough water to cover and bring to a boil, then reduce the heat, and cook, covered, for 15 minutes. Chop the cilantro leaves, then stir into the tagine together with the almonds and cook for a couple more minutes. Taste and adjust the seasoning. Serve garnished with the hard-cooked eggs and a lemon wedge on the side.

Duck noodles with ginger

Serves 2   *15 minutes preparation: 15–20 minutes cooking*

Slurpy noodle dishes are perfect quick, after-work suppers. All the supermarkets now sell a wide range of cooked noodles, ready to be slipped into a highly seasoned broth or piled into a wok for an impromptu stir-fry. Cooking your own noodles from scratch works out far cheaper than those ready-cooked packages and if you cook double the quantity you need, toss them with a little oil and stash the cooled noodles in a plastic bag or box in the refrigerator; they'll keep for a few days in perfect condition. This is one of those quick-and-easy noodle meal-in-a-bowl suppers for two that makes the most of ordinary, seasonal vegetables and one meaty duck fillet. A splash of soy sauce added to the broth and a generous seasoning of ginger and garlic add up to a very tasty and texturally interesting dish that is both satisfying and healthy.

5oz/150g dried egg noodles
1 leek or bunch scallions
1 carrot
1oz/25g piece fresh gingerroot
1 plump garlic clove
1 duck breast fillet

1 chicken stock cube
1 tbsp soy sauce
1 tbsp peanut oil
1 tbsp coarsely chopped cilantro
salt

Bring a large pan of water to a boil. Add the noodles and salt generously. Return to a boil and boil hard for 2 minutes. Drain, then return to the pan and cover to keep warm.

Meanwhile, trim the leek and slice thinly on the slant. If using scallions, trim and slice in long, thin, diagonal slices. In both cases include the green part that isn't tough and coarse. Peel the carrot and slice thinly on the slant. Peel the ginger and slice thinly, cutting it into small pieces. Peel the garlic and slice into paper-thin circles.

Slice across the duck fillet, cutting it into bite-size, thin strips. Dissolve the stock cube in generous 2 cups boiling water. Stir in the soy sauce. Heat a wok or skillet and, when very hot and beginning to smoke, add the oil, swirling it round the pan, followed by the leek, carrot, garlic, and ginger. Stir-fry for 5 minutes, keeping everything on the move so nothing burns, then add the duck.

Cook for an additional couple of minutes, or until the meat has all changed color. Add the stock and bring to a boil, then reduce the heat immediately and simmer for 10 minutes. Add the drained noodles, then stir well and simmer for a couple of minutes to heat through. Spoon into two suitable bowls and garnish with the cilantro, then eat with a fork and spoon.

Thai green duck curry with cilantro noodles

Serves 4   *15 minutes preparation: 35 minutes cooking*

Twenty years ago, very few people without the benefit of a Thai holiday would have come across satay, pad Thai, or green curry, or knew the meaning of sambal or would be familiar with the addictive flavors of lemongrass and cilantro. Today Thai food is increasingly popular, with its exotic flavors, fiery-hot curries, and coconut-milk gravies. The predominance of lightly cooked vegetables and seafood, and minimal use of meat, make it very much a cuisine of our times. The fresh pineapple is a delicious contrast which counteracts the chile heat beautifully.

2 skinless Barbary duck fillets, about 1lb/500g
1 garlic clove
3 shallots or 6 pink Thai shallots
scant ¾ cup fine green beans
8oz/225g canned sliced bamboo shoots in water
1 red chile
2in/5cm slice fresh pineapple, about 9oz/250g
1 tbsp vegetable oil

2 tbsp Thai green curry paste
14fl oz/400ml canned coconut milk
1 lemongrass stem
1 tbsp Thai fish sauce (*nam pla*)
1 lime
large handful coarsely chopped cilantro
7oz/200g rice sticks (tagliatelle-width rice noodles)
knob of butter

Get everything ready and assembled before you start cooking. Slice the duck across the grain into 2 x ½in/5 x 1cm strips. Peel and chop the garlic and shallots. Trim the green beans and halve. Rinse and drain the bamboo shoots. Trim the chile and split lengthwise, then scrape away the seeds and slice into long, thin strips. Chop into tiny dice. Remove the skin from the pineapple and cut into chunks, discarding the woody central core.

Heat a wok, large skillet or 8-cup-capacity pan and add the oil, curry paste, and 3 tablespoons of the coconut milk. Stir-fry for a couple of minutes, then add the garlic and shallots. Toss for another couple of minutes and add the meat, cooking for a few minutes until colored on all sides. Give the lemongrass a bash with a rolling pin to release its flavor and add that too, together with the fish sauce and remaining coconut milk.

Adjust the heat and let simmer, stirring occasionally, for 25 minutes, or until the duck is tender. Taste and adjust the seasoning with lime juice. Do not worry if the gravy seems very chile-hot. When the duck is tender, stir in the bamboo shoots, half the cilantro, and the pineapple. Heat through before transferring to a warmed bowl. Cover to keep warm. Cook the beans for 1 minute in boiling water. Drain. Place the noodles in a bowl, then cover with boiling water and let stand for about 4 minutes to hydrate. Drain. Toss with the knob of butter and remaining cilantro. Stir the beans into the curry and serve over the noodles.

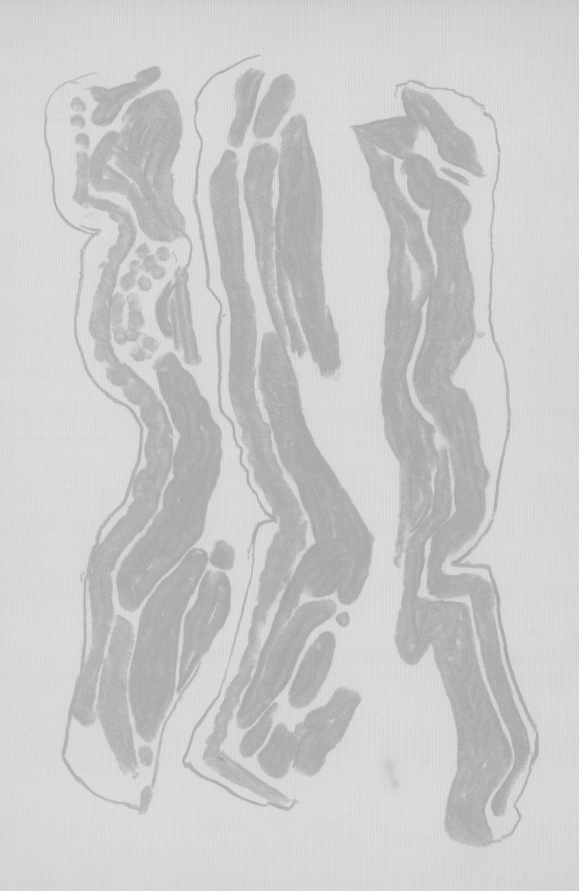

Pork, bacon, and ham

Pork can be utterly, utterly delicious, although it is famously difficult to cook well and can be disappointingly dry and tasteless. Some of the best pork dinners I've ever eaten have been at the hand of Chinese cooks because they understand the importance of pork fat. They cook their pork dishes gently and slowly and opt for the fatty cuts from the belly and neck end. Of all meats, the provenance of pork makes the greatest difference to the quality of its flavor and texture. It really pays to buy the best quality you can afford, although given the right cut with appropriate cooking, you can end up with a memorable dinner.

Shoulder meat is fattier than meat from the rear quarters and generally ends up tastier because the fat lubricates the meat as it cooks. It is also cheaper because most people think they want the lean, fast-cooking cuts from the middle (fillet and loin) and rear end (leg fillet and chops). The rib joint is also known as the collar joint and some butchers bone and roll it for roasting or pot-roasting. So-called barbecue ribs (very meaty) and belly slices (like very thick strips of bacon) are fatty but delicious and suit slow cooking. Surprisingly, they are also good steamed: simply cut the belly into chunks, then rub with seasoning and steam in a flat dish for about 10 minutes. The juices will mix with the melted fat to make a sauce. Pig's feet give stews a wonderful gelatinous texture. Although fatty, pork is a wet meat (like chicken, unlike lamb) and carries a lot of moisture. That's why joints shrink so during cooking. It also means it absorbs marinades easily. Stewing pork is usually diced shoulder—generally blade—boned and diced by the butcher. Fillet can be roasted whole but is best suited to thin slicing and brief frying, finishing perhaps with a dollop of mustard and cream. It is also useful for relatively speedily cooked stewy sorts of dishes.

When it comes to sausages, always choose ones with a high meat content— at least 70 percent. Cured sausage, such as highly seasoned chorizo and pepperoni, is a useful way of using a small amount of meat to inject plenty of flavor into quickly cooked stews, particularly those made with dried beans.

Angostura pork pot

Serves 4   *20 minutes preparation: 35 minutes cooking*

In Trinidad they splash Angostura—the "pink" in pink gin—into everything and it has an incredible power to "lift" certain foods. Shrimp, for example, tomatoes and chicken, and pineapple and banana are all perked up by a last-minute splash of Angostura bitters. I liked its effect so much that I wrote several recipes using it for my column in London's Evening Standard, *which inspired Angostura to ask me to write a recipe leaflet. This is one of them, a deliciously different, quick-and-easy, midweek supper for friends. Follow with vanilla ice cream splashed with Angostura. Or broil pineapple slices which you've drizzled with Angostura and sprinkled with brown sugar.*

1 large onion
3 garlic cloves
3 tbsp olive oil
14oz/400g pork
3½oz/100g sliced pepperoni
20 small new potatoes
14oz/400g canned chickpeas

generous 1¼ cups trimmed green beans
14oz/400g canned chopped tomatoes
2 tbsp Angostura bitters
Tabasco (optional)
2 tbsp coarsely chopped cilantro
salt and freshly ground pepper

Peel and halve the onion. Finely slice one half and finely chop the other half. Peel the garlic and slice into wafer-thin circles. Brown the onion in the oil in a large skillet or similarly wide-based, heavy pan placed over medium heat. Allow about 15 minutes for this, adjusting the heat so the onion doesn't burn. Stir in the garlic and cook for an additional 5 minutes.

While the onion and garlic are cooking, cut the pork into kabob-size chunks and cut the pepperoni in half. Meanwhile, cook the potatoes in salted boiling water. Tip the chickpeas into a strainer under cold running water and shake dry. Cut the beans in half. By now, the onion will be flopped and lightly browned. Push the onion to the side and brown the meat. Add the pepperoni. Cook for a couple of minutes, stirring so all the pepperoni comes into contact with the heat, then add the tomatoes and Angostura. Season with salt and pepper and stir thoroughly. Simmer for about 10 minutes, or until the pork is cooked through and the tomatoes have thickened and become saucelike.

Cook the beans in salted boiling water for 2 minutes. Drain. Add the drained potatoes and chickpeas to the stew and simmer until very hot. Taste and adjust the seasoning with salt and pepper. The pepperoni will give the tomato sauce a hit of chili, but if you want to make the dish hotter, add a few drops of Tabasco. Stir the cilantro into the stew. Serve with the beans.

Belly pork with sage, beans, and potatoes

Serves 4   *30 minutes preparation: 80 minutes cooking*

Belly pork looks like a thick strip of lean bacon. Inevitably it's very fatty, but the good news is that it's cheap and extremely tasty. Its French name—poitrine—sounds far more attractive and over there it's highly regarded for pâtés and terrines, for adding to stews, and making into rillettes. Four of these strips make a substantial stew, and in this one the meat is marinated in lemon juice, then cooked with crisply fried garlic. The garlic has a double role in that it flavors the oil in which all the other ingredients are cooked and the crisp flakes make an unusual garnish. Their slightly burned flavor and crisp texture provide a good contrast to the soft and mild textures and flavors of everything else. All you need with this hearty bowlful is some good crusty bread. Oh, and a brisk walk round the block afterward.

1 large unwaxed lemon
4 pieces belly pork or flank, about 2lb/1kg
2 large onions
3 garlic cloves
1 tbsp cooking oil
10 sage leaves, finely chopped
14oz/400g canned borlotti or other white beans

1¼ cups chicken stock, or ⅔ cup white wine
   and ⅔ cup water
1lb/450g Charlotte or other small, waxy potatoes
1 tbsp cilantro leaves
lemon wedges to serve
salt and freshly ground black pepper

Remove a paper-thin strip of lemon zest with a potato peeler. Place the pieces of meat on a plate and squeeze over juice from half the lemon. Peel and halve the onions, then slice. Peel the garlic and slice in very thin circles. Heat the oil in a skillet over medium heat and when hot, quickly stir-fry the garlic for a few seconds, letting it color and crisp. Remove from the skillet and drain on paper towels. Add the meat to the pan and brown for a couple of minutes on both sides. Return to the plate.

Now add the sliced onions to the skillet, then lower the heat and let them soften, adding the finely chopped sage and, after about 5 minutes, the lemon zest. Tip the beans into a colander and rinse under cold running water. Transfer the onions, sage, and lemon zest to a heavy-bottom, lidded casserole pan. Bury the meat in the onions and pour over any juices and the rinsed beans. Season thoroughly with salt and pepper and add the chosen liquid. Establish a simmer, then cover the pan and cook gently for 40 minutes.

Peel the potatoes and, when the cooking time is up, pile them into the pan. Squeeze over the juice from the remaining lemon half, then season again and cook for an additional 30 minutes. Remove the lid, then raise the heat and boil hard for 10 minutes. Stir in the cilantro, then sprinkle over the garlic and serve with lemon wedges.

Louisiana red beans and rice

Serves 2–3 *20 minutes preparation: 30 minutes cooking*

It always surprises me how much flavor a small amount of smoked bacon or smoked sausage can give to a dish. Polish kabanos are the secret ingredient of this unpromising-sounding Louisiana-style bean stew. Down South, they are very keen on combining onion with celery, usually with green bell peppers too, to give their dishes a fresh vivacity. Here the flavors are pepped up with chile and thyme and the hauntingly delicious beans are served over a mound of previously cooked rice and prettied up with chopped parsley. I like to serve it with my catering-size bottle of Tabasco and chilled beer.

1 cup basmati rice
1 onion
3 large garlic cloves
1 red chile (optional)
1 large celery stalk
5oz/150g smoked sausage such as Polish kabanos,
　or ham cut into chunks
1 tbsp cooking oil

1 bay leaf
2 tbsp chopped flatleaf parsley
1 tbsp chopped thyme
14oz/400g canned red kidney beans
½ chicken stock cube dissolved in 1¼ cups
　boiling water
salt and freshly ground black pepper

Wash the rice, then place in a pan with a well-fitting lid and cover with 1½ cups water. Allow to boil, then immediately turn down the heat and clamp on the lid. Cook for 10 minutes, then turn off the heat and let stand for 10 minutes for the rice to finish cooking in the steam.

While the rice cooks, prepare everything else. Peel and chop the onion and garlic. Split the chile, if using, then scrape away the seeds and chop into tiny dice. Peel the celery and slice across the stalk into very thin half moons. Chunk the sausage. Tip the rice into a bowl and keep warm. Wipe out the pan and add the oil. Place over medium heat and when the oil is hot, stir in the onion, garlic, and chile, if using, with the sausage, celery, and bay leaf. Cook briskly, stirring often, until the onion is soft and golden and the sausage has released some of its fat. Chop the parsley. Add the thyme and most of the parsley to the pan and season generously with salt and pepper.

Tip the kidney beans into a strainer and rinse with water. Shake dry and add to the pan. Now add the stock and adjust the heat so the stew simmers steadily for about 10 minutes. or until the liquid is reduced and looks more like a sauce. Taste and adjust the seasoning. Stir in the last of the parsley and serve over the rice.

Boston bean soup with watercress

Serves 4   *25 minutes preparation: 35 minutes cooking*

This is one of those useful recipes that relies on a couple of cans from the pantry and a few inexpensive easy-to-come-by ingredients. You end up with a thick and robustly flavored, satisfying soup; the sort of thing that people used to call a rib-sticker. It is even more special when served with a handful of freshly chopped tender green herbs and a generous grating of Parmesan stirred in right at the end. Watercress, or a mixture of flatleaf parsley, mint, and chives, gives the soup a noticeable injection of fresh flavor and vivacious color as well as a healthy dose of iron and vitamins.

2 tbsp olive oil, plus extra to serve
5oz/150g cubed pancetta or chopped lean bacon
1 large red onion
2 plump garlic cloves
3 carrots
2 celery stalks, with leaves if possible
½ tbsp all-purpose flour
1 tbsp smooth Dijon mustard
14oz/400g canned chopped tomatoes

1 chicken stock cube dissolved in 1¾ cups
   boiling water
squeeze lemon juice
½ tsp Tabasco sauce
14oz/400g canned cannellini or Great Northern
   beans
3oz/85g watercress
4 tbsp grated Parmesan cheese
salt and freshly ground black pepper

Heat the oil in a spacious, heavy-bottom pan over medium-low heat. Add the pancetta and cook until beginning to crisp. Meanwhile, peel and halve the onion, garlic, and carrots, then finely chop, keeping them in separate piles. When the pancetta is ready, stir in the onion and cook for about 6 minutes, or until floppy. Add the garlic and carrots. Season lightly with salt and generously with pepper. Cover and cook for 5 minutes, stirring occasionally, adjusting the heat so the vegetables sweat rather than brown.

Trim and finely slice the celery and its leaves and add to the pan. Cook for a minute or two, then remove the lid and sift the flour over the top. Stir until it disappears. Now stir in the mustard and add the tomatoes, a little of the stock, a squeeze of lemon juice. and Tabasco. Bring to a boil, gradually adding the rest of the stock. Tip the beans into a colander and rinse with cold water, then shake dry and add to the pan. Return to a simmer and cook for 10 minutes, or until the vegetables are tender.

Taste and adjust the seasoning. Finely chop the watercress. Just before serving, stir in the watercress and serve each portion with a spoonful of Parmesan and a splosh of best olive oil.

Huevos a la flamenca

Serves 2   *20 minutes preparation: 30 minutes cooking*

Tomatoes with eggs is one of my favorite combinations of food, and one which I like in many forms. This gutsy, robust tomato and egg dish is a specialty of Seville and it's something that everyone cooks slightly differently. I like it with chorizo and Spanish cured ham, as well as roasted piquillo peppers, and I've taken recently to cooking it with smoked as opposed to ordinary paprika. Peas give this combo a sweet freshness that works extremely well and the dish is uplifted with plenty of flatleaf parsley. The eggs are added right at the end and are poached in the stew until the white is set. Traditionally this is done in the oven, but I find it simpler to do over direct heat with a lid on the pan. Serve with plenty of crusty bread and butter. A cold beer or a bottle of a decent Rioja would be perfect accompaniments. Roasted piquillo peppers, stocked by most supermarkets, aren't essential to the success of the dish but enrich it greatly.

3½oz/100g sliced chorizo
4 slices Serrano or prosciutto
1 red onion
1 plump garlic clove
splash olive oil
1lb/500g fresh tomatoes or 14oz/400g canned
    chopped tomatoes

3 roasted piquillo pimiento red peppers
1 tsp sweet smoked paprika or regular "noble sweet"
    paprika
1 cup frozen baby peas (optional)
handful flatleaf parsley
4 eggs
salt and freshly ground black pepper

Choose a spacious skillet and gently cook the chorizo without any oil—it will produce plenty—until crusty on both sides. Make a pile of the ham, then fold it in half and slice thickly. Stir the ham into the chorizo. Remove the chorizo and ham to a plate, tipping the skillet so as much oil as possible remains in the skillet.

Meanwhile, peel and halve the onion and garlic, then finely chop. Add a splash of olive oil to the skillet and cook the onion and garlic for about 10 minutes, or until obviously beginning to soften. If using fresh tomatoes, pour boiling water over them. Count to 20, then drain, peel, and coarsely chop. Split the peppers, then scrape away the seeds and slice chunkily. Add the tomatoes, paprika, a generous seasoning of salt and pepper, and the piquillo peppers to the skillet and cook briskly for about 10 minutes, or until united into a thick sauce.

Return the chorizo and ham. Now add the peas, if using, and cook for 3–4 minutes, or until just tender. Coarsely chop the parsley and stir most of it into the stew. Make 4 indentations and crack the eggs directly into them. Cover the skillet and cook for about 5 minutes, or until the egg whites are just set. Serve immediately with the remaining parsley over the top.

Jambalaya

Serves 3–4 *20 minutes preparation: 50 minutes cooking*

Jambalaya is a rice, meat, and seafood stew from Louisiana. Traditionally the cooking starts with the so-called "trinity" of onion, green bell pepper, and celery which begins many dishes from the Deep South, but thereafter almost anything goes. The name is a jumble of jambon, *the French word for ham, and* alaya, *which means rice in an African dialect, and consequently the dish usually includes a spicy pork sausage of some sort, although often ends up with ham. Whatever the ingredients, a good jambalaya is always spiked with plenty of chile. My version of this easygoing dish is made even more colorful with red onions and red bell peppers and I have purposely restrained the chile-heat by using cayenne at the beginning of the cooking and adding Tabasco toward the end, while serving Tabasco and a wedge of lemon alongside so that people can adjust the dish to suit their own heat threshold. A good supply of ice-cold beer is essential.*

2 red onions, about 9oz/275g
2 plump garlic cloves
1 red bell pepper
1 celery heart
2 tbsp cooking oil
1 bay leaf
½ tsp cayenne pepper
2 large skinless boned chicken thighs
2 pepperoni sausages or 2oz/55g sliced chorizo

7oz/200g raw giant jumbo shrimp with shells
½ tsp Tabasco sauce
1¼ cups basmati rice
14oz/400g canned whole Italian tomatoes
1 chicken stock cube dissolved in generous
  2 cups water
1 tbsp finely chopped parsley
1 lemon (for wedges)
salt and freshly ground black pepper

Peel and chop the onions and garlic. Core, then deseed and dice the red bell pepper. Trim and slice the celery, setting aside the leaves, then rinse and drain. Heat the oil in an 8-cup heavy-bottom flameproof casserole dish and stir in the onion and garlic. Cook for about 5 minutes, then add the red bell pepper, celery, and bay leaf. Season with salt and pepper and cayenne and cook for about 10 minutes more while you prepare everything else.

Cut the chicken into chunks. Slice the pepperoni chunkily or halve the chorizo. If the shrimp are frozen, slip into warm water for about 5 minutes and remove the shells. Place the shrimp in a bowl and toss with the Tabasco. Stir the chicken into the vegetables and, when it's changed color, add the pepperoni (if using), the rice, and the canned tomatoes with their juice. Add the stock. Bring to a simmer, then cover the pan and cook for 20 minutes.

By now, the rice will have absorbed most of the liquid but the jambalaya should be nicely moist. If it isn't, add a little more stock. Stir in the shrimp, then cover the pan again and cook for 10 more minutes. Sprinkle over the celery leaves and parsley and serve with lemon wedges and the Tabasco bottle.

Chorizo and white bean stew

Serves 2   *15 minutes preparation: 15 minutes cooking*

In Barcelona's famous La Boqueria market, there is a fabulous little stall devoted to beans. White beans, black beans, kidney-shaped beans, and oval beans—it's hard to choose which ones to use for the inevitable chorizo or butifarra *stew. However, I turned to a can of cannellini beans for this approximation of a spicy Iberian bean stew. It's the sort of dish which can be expanded to fuel larger appetites or an extra mouth, by adding a few chunks of boiled potato. Serve hot from the pan with crusty bread and a chilled beer or lukewarm over shredded Boston lettuce hearts with a slice of garlic-rubbed toast drizzled with olive oil. Chilled dry fino or a glass of white wine would be my choice with the latter.*

2 strips rindless lean bacon
1 onion
2 plump garlic cloves
2 tbsp olive oil
1 bay leaf
2 tomatoes
14oz/400g canned cannellini beans

1 tsp chopped rosemary
½ tsp chopped thyme
1 tsp paprika
3 x 4in/10cm cooked chorizo
2 tbsp chopped flatleaf parsley
salt and freshly ground black pepper

Slice the bacon across the strips into strips. Peel and chop the onion. Peel and finely chop the garlic. Heat 1 tablespoon of the olive oil in a heavy-bottom medium-size pan placed over medium heat. Add the bacon and bay leaf and cook for a couple of minutes until the fat begins to run. Add the onion and cook, stirring frequently, for 3–4 minutes, adjusting the heat slightly so it browns without burning.

Chop the tomatoes. Tip the beans into a strainer and rinse thoroughly with cold water. Shake dry. Add the garlic, rosemary, and thyme to the pan and cook until aromatic. Stir in the paprika, then add the tomatoes. Cook, reducing the heat slightly, until the tomatoes have flopped to give a small amount of juice.

While that's happening, slice the chorizo in approximately ½ in/1cm-wide pieces. Add to the pan. Add the beans together with a generous seasoning of salt and pepper. Pour in scant ½ cup water and simmer for 5 minutes. Taste and adjust the seasoning. Stir in the parsley and the remaining olive oil. This stew will keep covered in the refrigerator for several days.

Oeufs landaises

Serves 2   *15 minutes preparation: 35 minutes cooking*

It was X. Marcel Boulestin, my eminent predecessor as cookery writer for the London Evening Standard, *who had the idea to call sausage hash* oeufs landaises. *He is one of my culinary heroes, with his conviction that good food should be a natural part of our daily life. He hated waste and believed in using up leftovers and eating seasonally. He also understood the importance of simplicity. This is my version of Boulestin's sausage hash.*

1 large onion	4 sage leaves or pinch dried sage
2 tbsp vegetable oil	2 eggs
6 good-quality pork sausages	handful grated Cheddar cheese
3 tomatoes	1 tbsp chopped parsley
8 small potatoes, boiled	salt and freshly ground black pepper
1 small apple	

Peel and halve the onion, then finely chop. Cook the onion in the oil in a skillet, cooking briskly and stirring often, until browned in places and beginning to soften—about 10 minutes.

Meanwhile, slash the sausages and remove the skin. Break them into small pieces. Place the tomatoes in a bowl and cover with boiling water. Count to 20, then drain. Cut out the core in a small cone shape and cut into fourths lengthwise. Scrape out the seeds and chop the tomato flesh. Chop the potatoes into chunky dice. Peel the apple and cut into fourths, then core and chop. Finely shred the sage, if using fresh leaves.

Add the pieces of sausage to the partially cooked onion, adjusting the heat and stirring occasionally so the sausage browns and cooks through. After about 10 minutes stir in the sage and add the potatoes. Cook for an additional 10 minutes, or until everything is browned, season with salt and pepper and add the tomatoes. Cook for 1 more minute. Season to taste with salt and pepper.

Break the eggs into the hash, then cover the skillet and return the skillet to the heat until the egg white firms. Sprinkle the cheese over the top. For a gratin finish, pop the hash under a preheated broiler; it is ready when the cheese begins to bubble but before the egg yolk hardens. Sprinkle with the chopped parsley and serve from the skillet.

Polish pork with pickled cabbage and dill

Serves 4 *20 minutes preparation: 45 minutes cooking*

Friday night, when for many the working week is over, is switch-off time. Sometimes it's just the ticket to slob around at home, cooking something easy to share with friends. Stewy dishes, the sort that simmer away on the back burner filling the house with good smells while you pour yourself a drink or two, always go down well. Often they are off-putting to make because they can take an age to cook. Not this one. It is also easy to shop for, mindless to prepare, and it reheats perfectly. This hauntingly flavored dish also manages to be both comforting and a bit special. Slices of crispy fried smoked pork sausage stirred into the thick, luscious, terracotta-colored sauce and a final garnish of sour cream with spikes of bright green dill, make this a supper you won't forget in a hurry. Serve alone with bread or make it go farther with mashed potato. You will definitely need a bottle of full-bodied red wine.

3oz/85g diced pancetta or smoked bacon pieces
2 tbsp shortening or vegetable oil
1 large onion
2 garlic cloves
2 pork shoulder steaks, about 1lb/500g
1 tsp caraway seeds
1 heaped tbsp sweet paprika

1 chicken stock cube dissolved in generous
 2 cups boiling water
1lb/500 jar sauerkraut
2 tbsp coarsely chopped dill
9½oz/275g carton sour cream
9oz/250g smoked pork sausage
salt

Choose a medium-sized, heavy-based pan and cook the bacon in 1 tablespoon of the shortening for about 5 minutes, or until crisp. Peel and dice the onion and garlic and add them to the pan. Cook, stirring occasionally, for 6–7 minutes, or until tender. Cut the pork into kabob-size chunks. Stir the caraway and diced meat into the pan and brown the meat all over. Add the paprika, cooking it for 30 seconds, and then add the hot stock. Bring to a boil, then reduce the heat immediately and simmer, covered, for 10 minutes.

Drain the sauerkraut and add it and 1½ tablespoons of the dill to the pan. Return the liquid to the boil, while stirring thoroughly, then reduce the heat and cook, covered, for 20 minutes, or until the meat and sauerkraut are tender. Stir ½ teaspoon salt and half the sour cream into the pan. Ten minutes before you're ready to eat, slice the pork sausage thickly and cook it briskly in the remaining shortening until nicely crusty. Stir the sausage into the stew, then check the seasoning and serve with a dollop of sour cream, garnished with the remaining dill.

Pork tenderloin with beer

Serves 4   *30 minutes preparation: 45–60 minutes cooking*

Pork can be annoyingly difficult to cook well. Too often it ends up dry, dull, surprisingly tough, and unimpressed by interesting flavor enhancers. One cut that's hard to spoil is pork fillet. Here, little scraps of lemon zest and occasional bursts of sage, with a background creaminess and heat from Dijon mustard, enliven what is essentially a gentle, comforting sort of dish. It doesn't really need an accompaniment, but you could add small, boiled new potatoes for the last 5 minutes of cooking, while mash is always good with a dish like this.

1 large onion	14oz/400g pork fillet
2 large garlic cloves	1 tbsp smooth Dijon mustard
8 large sage leaves	1 cup light beer
1 small unwaxed lemon	14oz/400g canned wax or cannellini beans
3 tbsp olive oil	salt and freshly ground black pepper

Peel and halve the onion, then finely slice. Peel the garlic and slice in wafer-thin circles. Place the sage leaves on top of each other and shred as thinly as possible. Remove the zest from the lemon in postage-stamp-size scraps without a hint of white pith. Heat the olive oil in a large skillet or a similarly wide-based pan and add the onion, garlic, sage, and lemon zest. Cook gently, stirring often, for at least 10 minutes, probably 15–20, or until the onion is floppy, golden, and scorched in places.

Meanwhile, cut the pork into large kabob-size pieces. Add the meat to the pan and increase the heat. Turn the pieces of meat regularly until browned all over. Season with salt and pepper and stir in the mustard. Add the beer, stirring as it comes to a boil, then reduce the heat so the liquid simmers very gently. Cover the pan and cook for 20 minutes.

Tip the beans into a strainer and rinse with cold water, then shake dry and add to the pan. Cook uncovered for 10 minutes or so to reduce and thicken the gravy. Taste and adjust the seasoning with salt and pepper if necessary before serving.

Portuguese pork

Serves 2   *15 minutes preparation: 20 minutes cooking*

The Portuguese are big on salt cod, chile, beans, and chickpeas. I've called this dish Portuguese pork because it is made with some of these ingredients and a few others that are popular in Portuguese cooking, such as garlic, onion, pork, and cilantro. It is a quickly made, fresh-tasting, and, above all, interesting stew which makes good use of pork fillet. I like to serve this with small new potatoes, cooked and then added to the pot at the end of cooking, but it is great as it is with a chunk of crusty bread. There again, rice would be good.

7oz/200g pork fillet
½ tsp ground cumin
juice of 1 small lemon
1 large red onion
3 tbsp olive oil
3 plump garlic cloves

1 small red chile
14oz/400g canned chickpeas
½ chicken stock cube dissolved in 1 cup boiling water
large bunch cilantro at least 3oz/85g
salt and freshly ground black pepper

Chop the pork into pieces slightly smaller than you would if you were making kabobs. Place in a bowl and sprinkle over the cumin. Squeeze over the lemon juice and toss. Peel and halve the onion, then finely chop. Heat the olive oil in a pan large enough to accommodate the entire dish over medium heat. Add the onion and cook, stirring every now and again, so that it softens and colors slightly. Cook for 10 minutes.

Meanwhile, peel the garlic and chop quite small. Split the chile, then scrape away the seeds and membrane and chop very small. Add the garlic and chile to the onion. Cook for an additional 5 minutes, stirring every now and again. Tip the chickpeas into a strainer, then rinse thoroughly with cold water and shake dry. Scoop the pork out of its lemon bath, then raise the heat slightly and stir it into the onion.

Stir constantly as the pork changes color. Add the chickpeas, stock, and cumin-flavored lemon juice left behind in the bowl. Bring everything to a boil and simmer gently, then stir well. Taste and season thoroughly (it will need it) with salt and pepper. Pick the cilantro leaves from the stems, then chop coarsely and stir into the stew. Simmer for a moment or two and serve.

Pork noodles with wilted spinach

Serves 4   *15 minutes preparation: 10 minutes cooking*

This simple, slurpy noodle supper is a good example of how easy it is to make quite ordinary, everyday ingredients into a healthy, delicious, and satisfying dish. The classic oriental trinity of garlic, chile, and ginger injects serious flavor, while rice wine and fresh cilantro combine with soy sauce to turn this quick and easy dish into a cross between a Vietnamese-style noodle soup-supper and a Thai stir-fry.

2½ cups chicken stock
7oz/200g dried rice sticks (tagliatelle-style)
1 bunch scallions, about 4oz/125g
1 plump garlic clove
1 small red chile
2in/5cm piece fresh gingerroot
7oz/200g pork scallop

generous 1 cup young spinach leaves
1½ tbsp sesame oil
2 tbsp sherry or rice wine
handful coarsely chopped cilantro leaves
soy sauce to serve
salt and freshly ground black pepper

Bring the chicken stock to a boil in a medium-size pan. Taste and season with salt and pepper. Soak the noodles, covered, for 4 minutes in boiling water. Drain, then add them to the simmering stock and cook for a couple of minutes. Turn off the heat and cover the pan.

Trim and slice the scallions, including all but the damaged or very tough green ends. Peel the garlic and chop finely. Split the chile and scrape out the seeds, then slice into thin batons and chop into tiny dice. Peel the ginger and grate or slice into very thin small batons. Slice across the grain of the scallops, cutting the meat into 1½in/3cm-long strips.

Bunch the spinach up in your hand and slice through it a few times to shred coarsely. Heat a wok or large skillet over high heat. Add the oil and swirl it round the pan. Lift the wok off the heat, then add the prepared scallions, garlic, chile, and ginger, and stir-fry for a few seconds before returning to the heat. Continue cooking for about 1 minute, reducing the heat so nothing burns, then add the strips of meat. Toss around for a couple of minutes, again adjusting the heat so the food cooks quickly but without burning. Add the sherry and allow almost to boil away until sticky. Stir the shredded spinach into the pan, tossing everything around for a few moments as the spinach wilts. Remove the wok from the heat.

Scoop the noodles into deep bowls and sprinkle with all but 1 tablespoon of the cilantro, but reserve about 1 tablespoonful. Pour on the stock and top with the meat and spinach mixture. Garnish with the remaining cilantro and serve with soy sauce, forks, and spoons.

Sausage and mushroom cassoulet

Serves 4   *15 minutes preparation: 25 minutes cooking*

This is nothing like a real cassoulet. There is no preserved goose in this version; in fact, the only common ingredients are sausages (which have a minor role in the Real Thing) and Great Northern beans. However, the dish looks somewhat similar and is grounded in the same sort of idea, whereby sausages and other ingredients are stewed together in a rich and robustly flavored wine gravy. This "cassoulet" is stunningly easy to make and is just the sort of stew-up that wards off the chilly blast of winter. If you are really big eaters, add some chunks of boiled potato and a handful of frozen peas. Serve in deep bowls and pass the mustard.

1lb/500g good-quality pork sausages
1 tbsp cooking oil (optional)
1 large red onion
2 plump garlic cloves
8 medium closed cap mushrooms
3 tbsp olive oil
1 bay leaf

1 tsp thyme leaves
2 glasses red wine, about 1¼ cups
squirt tomato ketchup
14oz/400g canned Great Northern beans
14oz/400g canned green lentils
squeeze lemon
salt and freshly ground black pepper

Begin by setting the sausages to cook in your favorite way. Don't prick them and if frying (in 1 tablespoon cooking oil) or broiling, cook over a moderate heat turning frequently as they begin to turn crusty and brown. Reckon on about 15 minutes' cooking.

Meanwhile, peel and halve the onion. Slice down the halves to make chunky half moons. Crack the garlic cloves with your fist, then flake away the skins and chop. Wipe the mushrooms and cut into fourths. Heat the olive oil in a skillet over medium heat and cook the onion, adding the garlic after 5 minutes. Add the mushrooms, bay leaf, and thyme leaves, then season generously with salt and pepper and continue to cook for an additional 5 minutes. Add the wine and ketchup and let it bubble up, then reduce the heat to a simmer.

Tip the Great Northern beans and lentils into a strainer and rinse under cold running water, then shake dry and add to the skillet. Season again and cook for 5 more minutes, or until the mushrooms are done to your liking. By now, the sausages should be ready. Add them whole to the stew or cut into small chipolata-size pieces. Taste and adjust the seasoning with salt, pepper, and a squeeze of lemon.

Spezzatino

Serves 4 *20 minutes preparation: 30 minutes cooking*

Pork fillet isn't the most economical cut, but it does always give good results. Take this Spanish-style stew. It's hard to believe that such a robust, full-bodied dish takes as little as 30 minutes to cook. It's one of those wonderful meal-in-a-bowl dishes that's full of lively, fresh flavors and the meat ends up tender and juicy. I like to serve it with plenty of crusty bread.

1lb/500g small new potatoes such as Charlotte
about 14oz/400g pork fillet
1 large red onion
1 red chile
1 large garlic clove
1 unwaxed lemon

3 tbsp olive oil
1¼ cups white wine or water
14oz/400g canned chickpeas
generous handful cilantro leaves
1⅔ cups young spinach
salt and freshly ground black pepper

Scrub or peel the potatoes and boil in plenty of salted water. Meanwhile, trim any fatty sinew from the pork and cut into kabob-size chunks. Peel and halve the onion and slice down the halves to make chunky half moons. Trim and split the chile and wipe away the seeds, then slice into small scraps. Peel the garlic and finely chop or slice into wafer-thin circles. Use a potato peeler to remove the zest from the lemon in paper-thin 1½in/3cm lengths.

Heat the olive oil in a spacious skillet or similarly wide-based pan and stir in the onion. Adjust the heat so it flops and softens, and browns in places without burning. After about 10 minutes, add the chile, garlic, and lemon zest and cook on, stirring often, for an additional 2–3 minutes, or until the garlic is aromatic and beginning to change color. Increase the heat slightly and cook the meat in batches, letting it brown all over before cooking the next batch. Adding it thus, instead of all at once, avoids the meat sweating instead of browning.

Return the browned meat to the skillet, then add the wine and cook at a steady simmer for 10–15 minutes, or until the meat is cooked through. Tip the chickpeas into a strainer and rinse under cold running water, then shake dry and add to the skillet. Heat through, then taste and adjust the seasoning with salt, pepper, and lemon juice. Coarsely chop the cilantro and stir it into the stew together with the spinach. By now the potatoes will be cooked. Drain them and add to the skillet. Stir and serve very hot as soon as the spinach has wilted.

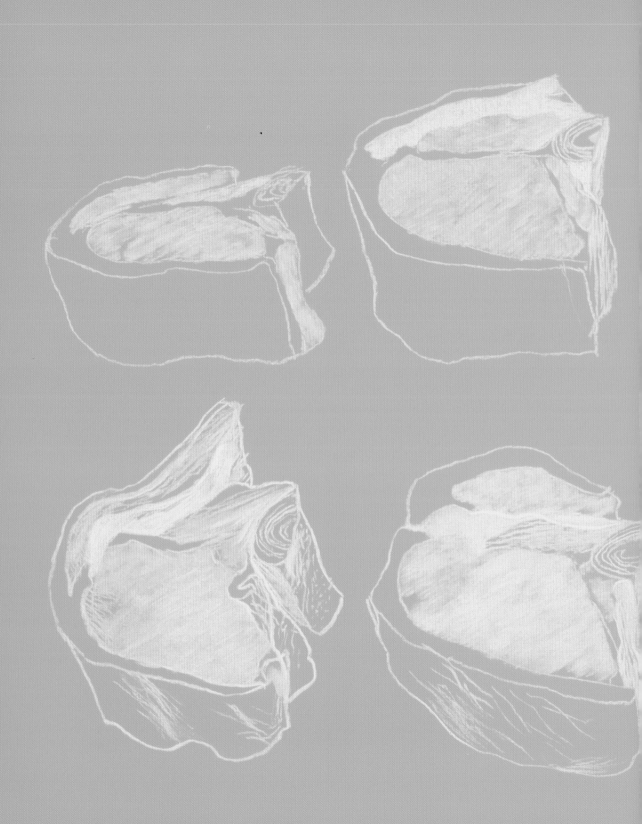

Lamb

It's hard to cook lamb badly. According to my butcher, the most popular cut is lamb fillet. It is ideal for quickly cooked dishes and perfect for kabobs because the fat running through it lubricates and flavors the meat. It is also a good but expensive choice for stewed dishes. Shoulder or neck slices are perfect for braising, and boned and diced, fat-trimmed shoulder meat is good for stews and casseroles. A proportion of bone gives the meat plenty of flavor, and the bony cuts of lamb are always the cheapest, but beware of splintery bones. Shanks provide plenty of delicious lean meat but are superb left on the bone and then cooked slowly, buried in a mound of finely sliced onion.

You can never go wrong with leg of lamb. Many people think they prefer it because it is far leaner than shoulder. It is usefully versatile and is as good for fast, pan-fried dishes as it is for slowly cooked stews and casseroles. Leg steaks and fillets can be delicious cooked simply and eaten in a meat-and-two-veg kind of a way. In summer it is worth looking out for salt-marsh lamb reared on coastal salt marshes. Its unique salty flavor is highly prized in France and a specialty from Mont St Michel in Normandy, where it's known as *pré-salé*.

I tend to buy loin chops, which are fatty but rich in flavor, for stews, and it's sometimes possible to pick up bargains at the supermarket on bumper packs of loin chops and neck slices. Having said that, I rarely buy lamb from the super-market. I prefer the wider selection of cuts and the freedom to buy the quantity that suits me and not the supermarket, which is offered by my butcher. All his lamb is free-range and properly hung, thus ensuring a robust lamby flavor and properly tender meat. Farmers' Markets are another excellent source of good-quality, often local, lamb.

Cocido of lamb with cilantro

Serves 4   *20 minutes preparation: 45 minutes cooking*

Cocido is the collective name for Spanish stews. They are cooked gently for several hours until the meat is tender and infused with flavor in a pot-bellied, earthenware crock with the equally distinctive name of olla. *Cocidos always include dried chickpeas and my after-work version speeds up the cooking with canned chickpeas. There's a background hint of heat from paprika and the stew is thickened and colored with canned tomatoes, then finished with shredded spinach and cilantro leaves. Serve it on its own with a chunk of bread. Boiled potatoes would be a good accompaniment too.*

2 garlic cloves
3 tbsp olive oil
1lb/500g boneless lamb leg steaks diced
1 red onion
14oz/400g canned chopped tomatoes
½ tsp paprika

1 tbsp tomato paste
14oz/400g canned chickpeas
5oz/150g young spinach leaves
generous handful cilantro leaves
salt and freshly ground black pepper

Peel and coarsely chop the garlic. Sprinkle it with a generous pinch of salt and use the flat of a knife to work to a juicy paste. Mix the paste with 1 tablespoon of the olive oil and smear the mixture all over the meat.

Let marinate while you peel the onion into fourths. Slice across the segments very thinly and cook in the remaining oil in a large skillet or similarly wide-based pan. Cook briskly, stirring often, for about 6 minutes, or until the onion is juicy, wilted, and beginning to brown. Season generously with salt and pepper, then turn down the heat and cook for an additional 4–5 minutes, then tip the juicy, browning onion onto a plate.

Return the skillet to medium-high heat and quickly brown the meat in batches so that it turns crusty rather than sweats in the skillet. Return the onion to the meat and add the can of chopped tomatoes. Give everything a good stir, scraping up all the crusty bits, then tip the stew into a heavy-bottom medium-size pan. Half fill the empty tomato can with water and add that to the pan together with the paprika and tomato paste. Bring the stew to a boil, then half cover the pan and simmer steadily for 20 minutes.

Tip the chickpeas into a strainer and rinse with cold water, then shake dry and add to the pan. Taste the juices and season with salt and pepper. Check that the meat is tender; if not, simmer for an additional 10 minutes or so. Shred the spinach, then coarsely chop the cilantro and stir both into the pan. When the spinach has wilted, the dish is ready.

Frito mallorquin

Serves 4 *20 minutes preparation: 45 minutes cooking*

The dish I kept hearing about on my first trip to Majorca was Frito Mallorquin. Properly made, it should include the full complement of lamb bits—the kidney, lungs, heart, and sweetbreads as well as the liver—and be thickened with its blood. But don't be alarmed: mine is a gentler version made only with the liver. I suspect it's one of those dishes that varies from cook to cook, but the basis for my recipe is the one I sampled at Jaume in Deia (which is an appetite-raising walk from Sa Padrissa, where I was staying). We ate it watching the sun go down on a terrace overlooking the curve of a mountain grounded by spots of light from the road. It's a hearty, robust dish by any standards, and not the sort of thing you expect to be eating after a day in the sun. But its juicy texture and complex flavors make it one of those meal-in-a-bowl dishes that is irresistible whatever the weather.

1lb/500g new potatoes
6 tbsp olive oil
3 large garlic cloves
1 red onion
1 bay leaf
14oz/400g lamb's liver
1 eggplant, about 14oz/400g
4 roasted piquillo pimiento red peppers or
  2 roasted red bell peppers

½ tsp chili flakes
generous pinch ground allspice or of cinnamon
  and cloves
8oz/225g shelled fava beans or fresh or
  frozen peas
1 tbsp chopped marjoram
salt and freshly ground black pepper

Scrub or peel the potatoes and boil in salted water until tender. Drain and cut into even-size chunks. Heat 3 tablespoons of the oil in a skillet and cook the potatoes slowly until crusty. Meanwhile, peel and finely slice the garlic. Peel and finely chop the onion. Heat the oil in a spacious flameproof casserole and stir in the garlic. Cook for a few seconds until aromatic, then stir in the onion. Add the bay leaf and cook, stirring occasionally, until the onion is soft.

Meanwhile, cut the liver into tiny dice; discard any sinew. Trim the eggplant and cut into dice about the size of sugar lumps. Split the peppers, then remove the seeds and chop into short strips. Stir the liver into the onions, then increase the heat and stir until it loses its pinkness.

Add the eggplant—it will seem an impossibly large amount, but soon softens and shrinks— and reduce the heat. Stir well, then add the chili flakes, allspice, and the peppers. Season generously with salt and pepper. Cover the casserole and cook for 20 minutes, or until the liver and eggplant are very tender.

Cook the beans in salted water for 3 minutes. Drain and, if liked (I do), remove their rubbery sheaths. If using peas, cook until just tender. Stir the beans and the potatoes into the casserole. Add the marjoram and serve.

Cumin lamb and eggplant stew

Serves 4   *25 minutes preparation: 35 minutes cooking*

If you're craving comfort food with attitude, I thoroughly recommend this Greek-inspired stew. Chunks of tender lamb fillet are hauntingly spiced with the unlikely-sounding combination of balsamic vinegar and cumin and held in a rich tomato sauce, which is thick with meltingly tender pieces of eggplant. This beguilingly flavored stew is lifted with the last-minute addition of fresh mint and offset by a scoop of creamy strained yogurt. In Greece they are very fond of serving stews with a tiny pasta called risi, named after its rice-like shape. Any of the small, so-called soup pastas would be perfect with this stew but, if you prefer, it goes very well with couscous or rice. Although the stew is relatively fast to cook, it is the sort of dish that improves with reheating and will probably taste even better tomorrow.

13oz/375g lamb neck fillet
2 heaped tsp ground cumin
1 eggplant, about 7oz/200g
1 large red onion
1 large garlic clove
2 tbsp olive oil

14oz/400g canned chopped tomatoes
1 tbsp balsamic vinegar
½oz/15g bunch fresh mint
⅔ cup strained plain yogurt
salt and freshly ground black pepper

Cut the lamb into chunks slightly smaller than kabob size. Dust with the cumin. Trim the eggplant and cut into similar-size pieces. Peel the onion, then cut in half and dice finely. Peel and finely chop the garlic. Heat the olive oil in a 8-cup-capacity, heavy-bottom, lidded pan and stir in the onion and garlic. Cook for 5 minutes over medium heat, stirring regularly.

Add the eggplant and quickly toss all the pieces in the oily onion. Reduce the heat and cook, stirring a couple of times, for 5 minutes, or until the eggplant begins to soften. Increase the heat and add the lamb, browning it thoroughly. Season with salt and pepper and add the tomatoes and balsamic vinegar. Half fill the empty tomato can with water and add that too. Bring to a boil, then reduce the heat immediately and three-quarters cover the pan to establish a steady simmer. Cook for 20 minutes.

Check the meat is tender and continue cooking for an additional 5–10 minutes if necessary. Coarsely chop the mint and stir most of it into the stew. Check the seasoning and serve with a dollop of yogurt and a sprinkling of the last of the mint.

Lamb and noodle stir-fry with ginger

Serves 2   *15 minutes preparation: 15 minutes cooking*

I have an on/off relationship with my wok. It hangs, unloved and gathering dust, for months on end and then for no apparent reason I use it night after night-after-night. Stir-fries, which are what most people use their wok for, never go out of fashion because they are quick, easy, and endlessly variable. This one is simply seasoned with the winning combination of garlic and ginger and given a Chinese imprint with sherry and soy sauce. Thai-style rice noodles, which need merely to be rehydrated before they are ready to eat, are perfect for quick stir-fries, but any noodles would work well.

6oz/175g rice sticks/rice noodles	2 large carrots, about 9oz/250g
9oz/250g boneless lamb leg steaks	4 tbsp sesame oil
1½ cups snow peas	1 tbsp sherry
1 leek	1 tbsp soy sauce
1 large garlic clove	handful cilantro leaves
2in/5cm piece fresh gingerroot	

Place the rice sticks in a bowl or pan and cover with boiling water. Let stand for 5 minutes, then rinse and drain. Slice the meat into thin strips of about 2in x ¼in/5cm x 0.5cm. Slice the snow peas on the diagonal into four pieces. Trim the leek and thinly slice on the diagonal; rinse and shake dry. Peel and finely chop the garlic. Peel the ginger and slice into skinny batons. Peel the carrots and thinly slice on the diagonal.

Heat 3 tablespoons of the oil in a wok or large skillet over the highest heat and swirl it round the pan. Add the leek, tossing it as it begins to wilt. Add the ginger and garlic and then the carrots. Stir-fry for a couple of minutes, then add the sherry and snow peas.

Keep the food moving for a couple of minutes, then scrape it to the side to make way for the meat. Add the remaining oil and the lamb. Cook without moving for a couple of minutes until crusty. Turn, cook for another 30 seconds or so, then sprinkle with soy sauce and mix with the vegetables. Add the cilantro and give one final toss, then turn off the heat. Drain the rice sticks, then pile into bowls and top with a share of the stir fry. Serve with soy sauce and, if you have some, a drizzle of toasted sesame oil.

Greek lemon lamb with new potatoes

Serves 4 *20 minutes preparation: 30 minutes cooking*

In Greece they are very fond of cooking lamb with lemon. The juice is squeezed over roasts and kabobs and combines with garlic and their fruity olive oil to make wonderful marinades. Lemon is also a useful ingredient to remember for ground lamb dishes. In this one, which was inspired by something similar I ate in Crete last year, lemon juice and zest permeate the lamb as it browns with scallions and a little garlic. Wilted young leaf spinach and grated zucchini turn the ground meat green and mint gives the finished dish a wonderful fresh flavor. Serve this tumble of delicious seasonal food over a mound of boiled new potatoes.

1lb/500g small new potatoes scrubbed	1 tbsp olive oil
1 bunch scallions, about 4oz/125g	¼ stick butter
1 plump garlic clove	1lb/500g good-quality ground lamb
1 unwaxed lemon	3 tbsp chopped mint
2 zucchini, about 4oz/125g each	2 tbsp strained plain yogurt or sour cream
1⅔ cups baby leaf spinach	salt and freshly ground black pepper

Boil the potatoes in salted water until tender. Drain and keep warm. Meanwhile, trim and finely slice the scallions. Peel the garlic and finely slice in circles. Remove a 2in x ½in/ 5cm x 1cm strip of wafer-thin zest from the lemon and chop very finely. Rinse and trim the zucchini and grate on the large hole of a cheese grater.

Put a second pan of water on to boil. When boiling vigorously, add the spinach. Bring back to a boil and cook for 30 seconds, then drain in a colander. Splash with cold water and press against the side to extract maximum water, then squeeze into a ball and chop coarsely.

In a heavy-bottom skillet or similar wide-based pan, heat the olive oil and butter over medium heat and stir in the scallions and garlic. After a couple of minutes raise the heat and add the meat, cooking until nicely browned. Season with salt, pepper, and the chopped lemon zest, then squeeze over the lemon juice. Cook until the lemon juice has amalgamated with the buttery meat juices and turned syrupy.

Stir in 2 tablespoons of the mint and the zucchini. Toss around for a few minutes until the zucchini begin to weep and soften but remain distinctive—don't overcook. Stir in the spinach and remaining mint. Reheat and stir in the Greek yogurt. Taste and adjust the seasoning. Serve the meat over the potatoes.

Harira

Serves 4–6 *20 minutes preparation: 40 minutes cooking*

*Harira is a thick and interesting Moroccan lamb and vegetable soup which is the official break-
fast after Ramadan. Flavored with saffron, cilantro, and flatleaf parsley, and finished with egg
and lemon juice, it is rich and aromatic, extremely satisfying, and very easy to make. My recipe
is adapted for speed and convenience.*

9oz/250g lean lamb such as fillet, or boneless leg
   or shoulder steaks
large knob butter
1 tbsp cooking oil
2 onions
2 celery stalks
1in/2.5cm piece fresh gingerroot
1 tbsp all-purpose flour
1 chicken stock cube
½ tsp saffron

2 tbsp chopped cilantro leaves
2 tbsp chopped flatleaf parsley
14oz/400g canned chickpeas
handful broken vermicelli or similar pasta
3 tomatoes
1 tbsp tomato paste
1 egg
juice 1 lemon
salt and freshly ground black pepper

Cut the meat into small kabob-size chunks. Heat the butter and oil in a spacious pan that
can accommodate the whole soup over medium heat. Brown the meat while you peel and
finely chop the onions. Add the onions to the crusty pieces of lamb and cook, stirring often,
for 6–7 minutes, or until the onions are limp and beginning to color. Finely slice the celery;
peel the ginger and grate or chop it. Add both to the pan and season with ½ teaspoon salt and
black pepper, then cook for a couple minutes. Stir in the flour until it disappears.

Meanwhile, dissolve the stock cube in 3½ cups boiling water and add it, together with the
saffron and herbs, to the pan. Increase the heat and stir as the soup comes to a boil. Reduce
the heat to a low simmer, then cover the pan and cook for 10 minutes. Tip the chickpeas into
a strainer and rinse under cold running water. Add the pasta and chickpeas to the soup, then
increase the heat and return to a boil.

Meanwhile, pour boiling water over the tomatoes and count to 20, then peel and chop. Add
the tomatoes and tomato paste to the soup and boil for 5 minutes, or until the pasta is tender.
Taste and adjust the seasoning. Whisk the egg, then add the lemon juice and stir into the
soup. Serve immediately or reheat as required without letting the soup boil.

Lamb and apricot tagine

Serves 4   *20 minutes preparation: 40 minutes cooking*

I make no claims for an authentic Moroccan recipe here, but the background flavorings of cumin, cinnamon, and saffron, with lemon juice, and a smear of hot harissa, are definitely reminiscent of the Real Thing and this is the perfect wintry after-work supper. If you prefer, you could replace the lamb with chunks of meat cut from skinned chicken thighs. Harissa, in case you're not familiar with it, is a fiery, terra-cotta-colored, chile-based paste, which is sold in cans, jars, and tubes and stocked by many supermarkets. It lifts the flavors wonderfully. In Morocco, tagine is served on its own, but couscous is the perfect accompaniment. Raisins, toasted almonds, and fried onions are all good additions too.

14oz/400g boneless lamb leg steaks
2 tbsp cooking oil
1 onion
1oz/25g blanched almonds
½ cup soft dried apricots
1 tsp ground cumin
1 tsp ground cinnamon
2 generous pinches saffron

1 chicken stock cube dissolved in 3½ cups
    hot water
1 small lemon
14oz/400g canned chickpeas
generous handful cilantro leaves
7oz/200g couscous
harissa to serve
salt and freshly ground black pepper

Cut the meat into even-size, small chunks. Heat the oil in a large skillet or similarly wide-based pan. When the oil is very hot, cook the lamb in batches so that it browns rather than sweats. Once it's browned—a couple of minutes a side—remove it to a plate.

Meanwhile, peel and halve the onion. Finely chop one half and thinly slice the other. Add the onion to the skillet and let it brown and wilt, adjusting the heat so it doesn't burn. After about 10 minutes, add the almonds and cook for a minute or so until lightly browned. Chop the apricots. Add the apricots, cumin, cinnamon, and 1 pinch of saffron. Stir well and cook for a few seconds before adding half the stock. Bring the liquid to a boil, then reduce the heat and simmer for 2 minutes before returning the meat and juice from half the lemon.

Tip the chickpeas into a strainer and rinse with cold water; shake dry and add to the stew. Coarsely chop the cilantro and add half to the skillet. Bring to a boil, then simmer, partially covered, for 15 minutes. Remove the lid, then taste and adjust the seasoning. Simmer for an additional 10 minutes, or until the meat is tender and the liquid reduced and thickened.

Meanwhile, bring the remaining stock to a boil and tip it into a serving bowl. Stir in the remaining saffron and the juice from the remaining half lemon. Add the couscous in a stream. Season with salt and pepper and stir. Cover and let stand for 15 minutes, or until all the liquid has been absorbed. Fluff the couscous with a fork. Stir the remaining cilantro into the tagine. Serve the tagine over a mound of couscous and daub sparingly with harissa.

Kheema matar

Serves 4–6   *20 minutes preparation: 60 minutes cooking*

Kheema *means ground lamb or beef and* matar *means peas, and that is exactly what this dish is: ground lamb with peas. It is one of the most delicious ways I know to combine those two ingredients, which, with a little help from Indian spices, chiles, and ginger, is particularly good when served over rice or scooped up in a paratha or rolled in a wrap. Kheema matar goes particularly well with mango chutney and something creamy such as strained plain yogurt or tzatziki, or cucumber raita made by grating or finely chopping cucumber into yogurt with some cilantro and a hint of chili powder.*

1 large onion, about 9oz/250g	1 tsp ground cumin
4 tbsp vegetable oil	½ tsp cayenne pepper
4 large garlic cloves	1 small lemon
1in/2.5cm piece fresh gingerroot	2½ cups frozen peas
2 small green chiles	large bunch cilantro
1lb 10oz/750g good-quality ground lamb	salt
1 tsp ground coriander	

Peel and finely chop the onion. Heat the oil in a wide-based pan that can hold all the ingredients and cook the onion over medium-low heat until tender and lightly browned. Meanwhile, peel and finely chop the garlic. Peel the ginger and grate or finely chop it. Split the chiles, then scrape away the seeds and chop finely.

When the onion is ready, add the garlic, followed by the chile and ginger. Cook for a couple of minutes before increasing the heat and adding the meat. Break it up with a wooden spoon and cook for about 5 minutes, stirring it every so often so that it browns evenly. Add the ground coriander, cumin, and cayenne. Stir well and cook for about a minute, then add ¾ cup water. Bring it to a boil. Immediately reduce the heat to very low, then cover the pan and cook for 30 minutes.

Add 1 teaspoon salt, the juice of half the lemon, ⅔ cup water, and the peas. Simmer, uncovered, for 5–10 minutes, or until the peas are tender. Meanwhile, coarsely chop the cilantro—you need approximately 4 tablespoons—and stir it into the meat when the peas are cooked. Taste and adjust the seasoning with salt and lemon juice. Scoop the mixture into a warmed serving dish, leaving behind the fat that will have accumulated.

Irish stew

Serves 6 *20 minutes preparation: 90 minutes cooking*

I'm not Irish, but with an Irish builder in what seems like permanent residence, I'm beginning to feel it. He's a bit special, is Dermot. And he likes to cook. He reckons that this recipe makes the best Irish stew he's ever eaten, which is praise indeed from a Dubliner. I'm quite surprised by this because I make it with supermarket chops instead of mutton and King Edward potatoes instead of creamy Irish potatoes. In my version, I leave the carrots in big chunks, add masses of onion, and season the stew with plenty of salt, pepper, a sprig or two of thyme, and a large quantity of curly parsley to really lift the flavors. The knob of butter added at the end of cooking gives the gravy sheen and body, adding a touch of luxurious creaminess. It is delicious served with hunks of bread and some peas.

2lb/1kg lamb chops or lamb shoulder, neck,
   or loin chops
6 large carrots
6 onions
12 potatoes

6 sprigs thyme
knob cold butter
3 tbsp finely chopped curly parsley
salt and freshly ground black pepper

Trim the bulky fat off the lamb. Peel the carrots and cut each into three—you want big chunks. Peel the onions and cut into fourths, then halve each segment lengthwise. Peel the potatoes and let soak in cold water.

Choose a spacious heavy-based flameproof casserole or pan with a tight-fitting lid and cover the base with half the chops. Season generously with salt and pepper and half the thyme. Spread half the carrots and onions over the meat. Season again and repeat. Pour 2½ cups water over the stew and bring to a boil. Establish a very low simmer, then cover the dish and cook for 40 minutes.

Drain the potatoes, then pile over the stew and season thoroughly. Return the lid and cook for another 40 minutes, or until the potatoes are tender but firm. Cut the butter into pieces into the stew. Add most of the parsley and gently stir until the butter has dispersed. Sprinkle over the last of the parsley and serve.

Lamb and barley broth

Serves 2–4   *20 minutes preparation: 40 minutes cooking*

This old-fashioned lamb and pearl barley soup-cum-stew smells lip-smackingly good as it simmers away in the background while you get on with something else. The medley of vegetables —yellow rutabaga, orange carrots, and bright green peas—and vivacious garnish of parsley, are extremely appetizing. There is plenty here for two meal-size bowlfuls for two hearty eaters but sufficient quantity for three or four "normal" ones. Quantities are easy to scale up and the soup reheats perfectly.

1 onion
½ tbsp vegetable oil
2 carrots
1 small rutabaga, about 10oz/300g
13oz/375g shoulder of lamb chops or other stewing
　lamb
generous ¼ cup pearl barley

½ tsp fresh thyme or ½ tsp dried
1 chicken stock cube dissolved in scant 3 cups
　boiling water
2 scallions
1 cup frozen peas
1 tbsp chopped parsley
salt and freshly ground black pepper

Peel and halve the onion, then finely slice. Heat the oil in a medium-size, heavy-bottom pan and cook the onion gently, stirring occasionally, while you prepare everything else. Peel the carrots and slice quite thinly. Peel and halve the rutabaga and chop in sugar-lump-size dice. Trim the lamb of excess fat and skin and cut it into small chunks slightly smaller than you would for kabobs. Wash the pearl barley until the water runs clean.

Stir the meat into the onion, then increase the heat and quickly brown it all over. When no red remains, season with ½ teaspoon salt and plenty of pepper. Add the thyme, carrots, and rutabaga and stir thoroughly. Cook for a couple of minutes, then add the pearl barley. Now add the stock and bring the soup to a boil. Turn down the heat immediately and skim away the brown foam that will form as best you can; leftovers will soon disperse and won't spoil the flavor of the soup. Partially cover the pan and leave at a low simmer for about 25 minutes, or until the pearl barley is puffed (like puffed wheat) and almost tender.

Trim and slice the scallions. Add the scallions and peas to the pan, then increase the heat slightly and cook, uncovered, for about 5 minutes or until the peas are tender. Taste and adjust the seasoning with salt and pepper. Stir in the parsley and serve.

Burmese lamb and potato curry

Serves 6   *30 minutes preparation: 50–60 minutes cooking*

Over the years, my friend Eddie Lim has often mentioned his Burmese curry. When I eventually tasted it and later cooked it myself—several times—I can see why. It is such a simple recipe. So delicious. And so impressive. The secret of the dish is to cook the onion, garlic, and ginger paste until it is dry and beginning to brown, and to seal the meat thoroughly. This results in a rich, thick, rust-colored, soupy gravy, which is hauntingly subtle but with sufficient chile heat to make it interesting without blowing your head off. It is worth mentioning that this curry is also very good made with chicken or a mixture of root vegetables with a few green beans or broccoli added at the end. It is served over noodles in deep soup bowls with a garnish of cilantro leaves.

6 large garlic cloves
2 large onions
1oz/25g piece fresh gingerroot
5 scant tbsp olive oil
1 tsp paprika
2 tsp chili powder
generous pinch of saffron dissolved in 1 tbsp
   boiling water
2 tbsp Thai fish sauce (*nam pla*)

1lb 6oz/625g casserole lamb or boneless leg
   steaks diced
1lb/500g small waxy potatoes, peeled
4 cups chicken stock
1lb/500g Chinese or Thai rice noodles
few sprigs cilantro
salt

Peel the garlic and onions, and chop the ginger coarsely. Place the ginger and garlic in the bowl of a food processor and blitz. When finely chopped, add the onions and blitz briefly until finely minced.

Heat 3 dessertspoons of the olive oil in a spacious heavy-bottom pan and, when very hot, stir in the onion mixture. Reduce the heat and cook, stirring often, for 20–30 minutes, or until dry, brown in patches, and pastelike. Add the paprika, chili powder, saffron, and fish sauce. Cook, stirring constantly, for 30 seconds. Brown the lamb in uncrowded batches in the rest of the oil in a skillet. Add the lamb and peeled potatoes to the paste. Add the stock. Bring to a boil, stirring frequently, and simmer for approximately 30 minutes, or until the meat is tender.

Taste and adjust the seasoning with salt. Five minutes before you are ready to serve, soak the noodles in boiling water. Serve the curry and its soup over the drained noodles and garnish with a few sprigs of cilantro. This curry reheats brilliantly.

Lamb provençal

Serves 4   *20 minutes preparation: 35 minutes cooking*

When a dish is described as à la niçoise *or* à la provençale, *it is made with a chunky tomato sauce cooked with garlic, often with onions, and sometimes with olives, anchovies, and eggplants. The niçoise version tends to be the more elaborate of the two and might also include capers, artichokes, and zucchini. Basil is likely to appear in both and tarragon might be included too. Both sauces are a celebration of local vegetables and flavorings and are liberally interpreted according to what is available. Black olives always appear in niçoise sauces but come and go in provençal versions. Rice is the traditional accompaniment to a provençal dish but new potatoes —boiled first and added at the end of cooking—or green beans and a chunk of bread to mop up the wonderful tomato sauce go very well too. The anchovy, incidentally, is used instead of salt and adds a wonderful depth of flavor which is not the least bit fishy.*

2 onions, about 10oz/300g
3 tbsp olive oil
2 red bell peppers
1 bay leaf
2 garlic cloves
2lb/1kg lamb fillet
5 large tomatoes, about 1lb 6oz/625g

1 tsp anchovy extract or 2 canned anchovy fillets
  (optional)
about 20 black olives (optional)
handful basil leaves (optional)
juice ½ lemon
salt and freshly ground black pepper

Peel and halve the onions, then finely slice. Add 2 tablespoons of the olive oil to a lidded pan that can hold all the ingredients. Stir in the onions, then cover the pan and cook over medium heat for 5 minutes. Meanwhile, use a potato peeler to peel the red bell peppers. Don't be too finicky about this; you just want to get rid of most of the skin. Cut the peppers into fourths lengthwise. Scrape out the seeds and white membrane and slice across the pieces to make strips. Stir the red bell peppers into the softened onions and cook for 10 minutes, uncovered, adding the bay leaf, and the garlic as soon as you have peeled it and finely sliced in circles.

While that is going on, trim the lamb fillet and cut into kabob-size pieces. Place the tomatoes in a bowl of boiling water. Count to 20. Drain the tomatoes, then peel and coarsely chop. Push the onions and bell peppers to the side of the pan. Raise the heat and add the remaining olive oil. When very hot, add the meat. Quickly brown it before stirring everything together. Add the anchovy extract or fillets, if using, mashing up the fillets so they dissolve into the sauce, and season with pepper. If not using anchovy, season with salt too.

Add the tomatoes and simmer uncovered for 20 minutes, or until the meat is cooked and the tomatoes have turned into a sauce with the onions and peppers. If it seems too watery, increase the heat to boil off some of the liquid. If including olives and/or basil, add now. Taste the sauce and adjust the seasoning with salt, pepper, and lemon juice. This dish reheats well.

Aromatic lamb curry with spinach

Serves 4 *25 minutes preparation: 40 minutes cooking*

If you are a curry novice, this is an excellent recipe to cut your teeth on. I like the fact that it doesn't take hours to cook and that the flavors end up fresh and interesting rather than blowing your head off with fiery heat. It looks pretty too, the thick creamy sauce flecked with chunks of tomato and spinach. Serve it with rice or warm naan bread with a full complement of curry add-ons—poppadoms, lime pickle, and raita.

3 large garlic cloves

2in/5cm piece fresh gingerroot

1 green chile

5 tbsp strained plain yogurt

1 tsp ground cumin

1lb/500g boneless leg or shoulder lamb steak diced

1 large onion

2 tbsp vegetable oil

1 tsp ground coriander

1 bay leaf

4 cloves

seeds from 4 cardamom pods

7oz/200g young spinach leaves

4 medium tomatoes

generous pinch cayenne or mild paprika

salt

Peel and chop the garlic and ginger. Split the chile and discard the seeds, then chop. Pound these ingredients together to make a paste. Tip the yogurt into a mixing bowl and whip with half of the ground cumin. Add the paste and meat, then stir well and let marinate while you peel and chop the onion.

Heat the vegetable oil in wide pan until very hot. Stir in the onion and cook for a couple of minutes before reducing the heat, sprinkling with ½ teaspoon salt, the remaining cumin, the coriander, bay leaf, cloves, and cardamom seeds. Stir thoroughly, then cover the pan and cook for 10 minutes, or until the onion is juicy and lightly colored.

Meanwhile, bring a large pan of water to a boil. Drop in the spinach and return to a boil. Cook for 20 seconds, then scoop out of the pan into a colander. Drop the tomatoes into the boiling water. Count to 10 and remove, then peel and chop. Press the spinach against the side of the colander to drain, then chop. When the onion is ready, increase the heat and add the meat and its yogurt marinade to the pan. Cook briskly so that the meat browns all over and the yogurt thickens.

Sprinkle with cayenne and stir in generous ¾ cup boiling water, ½ teaspoon of salt, and the chopped tomatoes. Bring the curry to a boil, then reduce the heat immediately and simmer, covered, for 20–30 minutes, or until the meat is tender. Stir in the spinach and heat through, then serve.

Lamb, chickpea, and potato hash

Serves 3–4   *20 minutes preparation: 25 minutes cooking*

Comfort food with attitude is how I would describe a bowl of this hash. It is made with the vital ingredients for hash—onions and potatoes—but the protein element, which in this case is ground lamb, comes with layers of interesting extra flavors.

1lb/500g new potatoes
1 large red onion
2 tbsp cooking oil
2 garlic cloves
1 unwaxed lemon
1 tsp thyme leaves
14oz/400g canned chickpeas
2 tbsp chopped flatleaf parsley

9oz/250g ground lamb
½ chicken stock cube dissolved in ⅔ cup
   boiling water
1½ tbsp chopped mint
Tabasco sauce (optional)
1 cups frozen peas
salt and freshly ground black pepper

Put the potatoes on to cook in plenty of salted boiling water until tender. Drain. Return to the pan with cold water to cover and let stand for about 30 seconds to cool. Drain again and whip off their skins. Cut the potatoes into chunky wedges by cutting them into fourths lengthwise.

Meanwhile, halve and thinly slice the red onion. Heat the oil in a large skillet or large shallow pan. Cook the onion until soft and slippery—about 10 minutes. While the onion is cooking, peel and chop the garlic and use a potato peeler or zester to remove the lemon zest in wafer-thin sheets. Chop the zest very finely. Coarsely chop the thyme leaves. Tip the chickpeas into a strainer, then rinse well with cold water and shake dry.

Add the garlic, lemon zest, thyme leaves, and half the parsley to the pan and stir everything around until the garlic is aromatic. Add the ground lamb and stir-fry until the meat changes color from pink to brown. Add the stock, the mint, a shake of Tabasco, if you like a hint of chili zing, and let everything bubble up together for a couple of minutes. Add the chickpeas and juice from half the lemon and the potatoes. Season generously with salt and black pepper and simmer for 10 minutes so the potatoes get a chance to soak up some of the delicious juices and become very hot.

Add the peas and cook for a minute or two until they are tender. Squeeze juice from the remaining lemon half over the top and stir, then taste and season again with salt and pepper as necessary. Garnish with the last of the parsley.

Lemon and rosemary lamb with cannellini beans

Serves 2   *20 minutes preparation: 40 minutes cooking*

Lemon zest, garlic, and rosemary are a wonderful trinity that often features in Italian cooking. I particularly like it with dried beans—everything chopped small, then fried with a chopped onion before adding the soaked beans—and would recommend it as a way of livening up a can of cannellini or one of the other similar green or white beans. That was the thinking behind this meal-in-a-bowl, which was inspired by the need to use a small amount of meat to good effect without it seeming mean. Being something of a carbohydrate junkie, I like to add boiled new potatoes to dishes like this. You may prefer to leave them out and serve a big bowl of green beans instead.

1 unwaxed lemon	5oz/150g boneless lamb loin
1 large red onion	2 glasses red wine, about 1¼ cups
4 large garlic cloves	1 tbsp tomato paste or ketchup
2 tsp rosemary leaves	14oz/400g canned cannellini beans
3 tbsp olive oil	2 tbsp parsley
1 bay leaf	salt and freshly ground black pepper

Use a zester or potato peeler to remove four long, wafer-thin strips of zest from the lemon. Tear into small scraps. Peel and halve the onion, then finely chop. Peel the garlic and slice in wafer-thin circles. Very finely chop the rosemary leaves. Heat the olive oil in a medium-size pan with a heavy base. Add the onion, lemon zest, bay leaf, and rosemary, and cook, stirring every now and again, over medium heat for about 10 minutes, or until the onion is softening and beginning to brown. Add the garlic and cook for a few more minutes.

Meanwhile, slice the meat into skinny strips, approximately 2in x ½in/5cm x 1cm. Clear a space in the middle of the aromatic, browned onion and brown the meat as best you can. Mix the onions into the meat and season generously with salt and pepper, then add the red wine and tomato paste. Bring to a boil, then reduce the heat immediately and simmer for about 15 minutes.

Meanwhile, tip the cannellini beans into a strainer and rinse under cold running water. Shake dry. Coarsely chop the parsley. Add the beans and half the parsley to the meat and onion. Simmer, crushing the beans slightly with the back of a wooden spoon, and cook for about 10–15 minutes, or until everything is very hot, the meat cooked through, and the juices are moist but not too wet.

Taste and adjust the seasoning with salt, pepper, and lemon juice. Stir in the rest of the parsley. If adding potatoes, cook them separately in salted boiling water and stir them into the stew just before serving.

Moroccan meatballs with peas

Serves 2   *30 minutes preparation: 35 minutes cooking*

If you wanted to eat traditional Moroccan food, as opposed to Frenchified international stuff, at the hotel where I once stayed in Taroudant, it had to be ordered after breakfast. I was determined to try everything, but each meal was so good that every day I was torn between re-ordering what we'd eaten the night before and taking a chance. The bisteeya, *or* pastilla *as it's more commonly known, was wonderful; it's a flaky, pastry pie stuffed with pigeon and almonds, and I nearly asked the kitchen to make one for me to take home. I couldn't resist ordering sweetbreads with preserved lemon and cilantro three days running. By comparison, meatballs didn't sound exciting, but I am so glad we tried them. That night, they were made with ground lamb flavored with cumin and mint, and served in an onion gravy made aromatic with* ras el hanout *(the national spice mix) and sweetened with golden raisins and honey. Bobbing in the gravy, adding a fresh lively contrast, were peas and chopped mint. If you cannot find* ras el hanout, *make do with a pinch each of ground mace, cinnamon, nutmeg, cloves, allspice, and black pepper.*

2 red onions
1 tbsp cooking oil or half butter and half oil
½ tsp *ras al hanout*
2 tbsp golden raisins
½ tbsp runny honey
½ chicken stock cube dissolved in 1¼ cups
    boiling water

about 25 mint leaves
9oz/250g ground lamb
½ tsp ground cumin
1 egg yolk
2½ cups frozen peas
squeeze lemon
salt and freshly ground black pepper

Peel and halve the onions. Finely slice three of the halves. Heat the oil in a deep skillet or large, shallow pan over high heat. Toss the sliced onions around for a few minutes until beginning to color. Add the *ras al hanout*, golden raisins, honey, and 1 cup of the stock. Bring to a boil, then reduce the heat so the liquid simmers. Cover the skillet and cook for 15 minutes. Remove the lid and cook for a few minutes until the onions are soft, the golden raisins plump, and the liquid reduced to make a juicy gravy. Salt generously.

Meanwhile, grate the reserved onion half. Chop the mint. Place the lamb in a mixing bowl. Add the grated onion, half the chopped mint, the cumin, a good seasoning of salt and pepper, and the egg yolk. Mix well, mulching together with your hands, forming the mixture into a ball. Rinse your hands and shake dry, then pinch off lumps of the mixture to roll around between your hands to make balls the size of cherry tomatoes. You should end up with about 30 balls.

Add the remaining stock to the gravy, then bring back to a boil and add the meatballs. Adjust the heat so the gravy bubbles gently over the balls, letting them darken and firm. Roll them around so they cook evenly, then add the peas and remaining mint and cook until tender. Taste and adjust the seasoning with salt, pepper, and a squeeze of lemon. Serve hot or lukewarm.

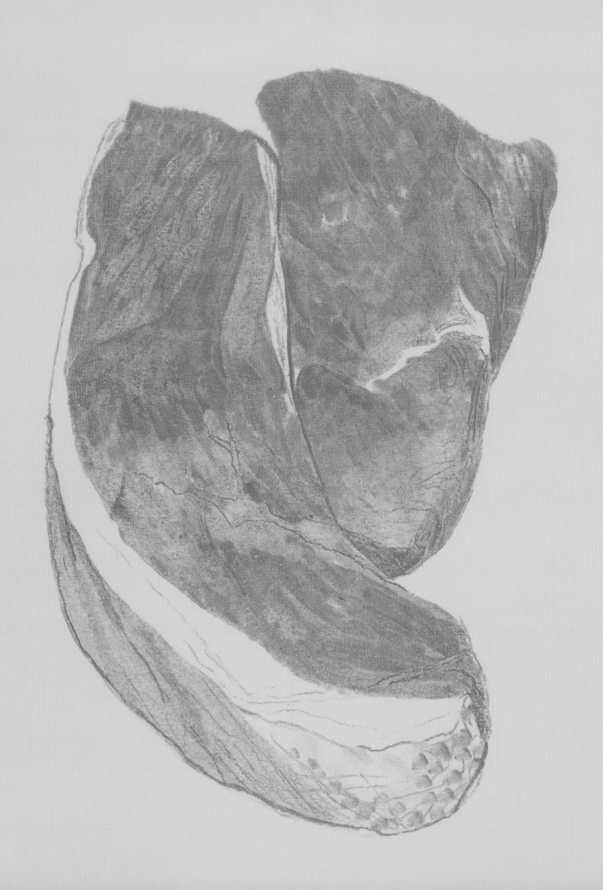

Beef, veal, and venison

Nothing beats the flavor and texture of a fine piece of beef. It doesn't matter which cut you chose; as long as it is cooked appropriately, there is nothing comparable. Quickly cooked dishes, like stir-fries and pan-fried recipes, need lean cuts from gently worked muscle like melt-in-the-mouth tenderloin steak and fat-marbled sirloin steak, which embraces entrecote, T-bone, and porterhouse steaks. These are all found in the middle of the beast, flanked by the forerib. This is the ultimate joint to roast for flavor and tenderness. Best value for fast cooking are the minute rump steaks and a clutch of shoulder steaks with distinctive ridged meat and curious names like bollo, skirt or *bavette* (the French name), and feather, or the similar French cut called *onglet,* which has gristle running down the center. It's rare to find these cuts in the supermarket, but any butcher worth his salt will be happy to oblige—if he hasn't already nobbled them for his regulars. All these cuts are good for long, slow dishes too, but will be tough if not cooked until the fibers break down and the meat becomes meltingly soft. The fore-quarters of the beast— the shoulders and lower legs, which are the parts that have been worked the hardest—are the best for stewing. These tougher cuts, such as clod, foreshank, chuck, and blade, have plenty of flavor but need long, gentle cooking.

These days, in the wake of BSE and the devastation that followed the outbreak of foot and mouth disease which spread through British beef production, we are all very conscious of the heritage of the meat we eat. We can now buy organic and certifiable beef in the supermarket and are learning to realize that properly reared meat, particularly beef, is never going to be cheap. I don't eat beef that often, and when I do, I buy it from my butcher who specializes in Scottish grass-reared beef.

Venison has become a popular alternative to beef. Many people are worried about eating veal because of the cruelty involved to achieve pale meat, but it is now possible to buy humanely reared veal.

Chilean beef stew with corn

Serves 4   *25 minutes preparation: 65 minutes cooking*

Variations on this colorful and interesting stew are plentiful in Chile. Sometimes it's made with lamb and flavored with ground cumin, while the beef version is usually seasoned with paprika to give it a rich, spicy finish. For a luxurious, creamy gravy, it is sometimes finished with beaten egg stirred into the stew just before it's served.

1 onion
1 bay leaf
2½ tbsp vegetable oil
2 tsp dried oregano
9oz/250g peeled pumpkin
1 leek
2 carrots
14oz/400g beef sirloin or other tender fillet diced

1 tbsp paprika
2 cups corn kernels
1lb/500g small new potatoes
1 chicken stock cube dissolved in generous
   2 cups boiling water
1 tbsp chopped parsley
salt and freshly ground black pepper

Peel and dice the onion. Place the onion and bay leaf in a spacious heavy-bottom pan with 2 tablespoons of the vegetable oil and stir in the oregano. Cook over medium heat for 5 minutes while you cut the pumpkin into kabob-size chunks. Stir the pumpkin into the onion and season with salt and pepper, then cover the pan and cook for an additional 5 minutes. Trim and slice the leek. Rinse under cold running water and shake dry. Peel the carrots and cut into chunky circles. Stir the leek and carrots into the onion, then cover and cook for an additional 5 minutes.

Dust the meat with paprika. Clear the vegetables to the side of the pan and add the remaining oil, then increase the heat and add the meat. Brown the meat, then add the corn, potatoes, and chicken stock. Bring to a boil, then reduce the heat so the stew simmers steadily and cook, covered, for 45 minutes, or until the meat is tender. Adjust the seasoning with salt and pepper, then stir in the parsley and serve.

A quick and luscious beef stew

Serves 2   *20 minutes preparation: 40 minutes cooking*

This is the perfect recipe for the times when you want the comfort of a good old-fashioned stew but haven't the time to make it properly using one of the more appropriate cuts, such as chuck or foreshank, that need long, slow cooking. Separately boiled new potatoes—which could be boiled in the pan before you cook the stew—could be added to the pot at the last minute, or you may prefer to eat it with mash over a doorstep of white bread.

3 strips lean bacon
1 large onion, about 10oz/300g
2 large portobello mushrooms
10oz/300g tender, lean frying steak
1 heaped tbsp all-purpose flour
2 tbsp cooking oil
1 bay leaf
1 glass red wine

1 scant tbsp red currant jelly
½ chicken stock cube dissolved in 1½ cups
   hot water, or water
3 carrots
1 cup frozen peas
½ tbsp chopped parsley
salt and freshly ground black pepper

Chop the bacon into lardons. Peel and halve the onion, then dice one half and slice the other. Slice the mushrooms. Trim the meat and slice it across the grain in thin diagonal strips. Place the meat in a bowl and toss with the flour. Over a low-medium flame, heat half the oil in a heavy-bottom pan that will be able to accommodate all the ingredients. Cook the bacon until beginning to crisp, then add the onion with the bay leaf. After about 5 minutes, when it's starting to look juicy, add the sliced mushrooms and a generous seasoning of salt and pepper. Stir occasionally so the mushrooms cook evenly and, after a few minutes, tip the contents of the pan onto a plate.

Lower the heat, and heat the remaining oil in the pan. Add the meat and all the flour, stirring it around. Cover the pan and let stand for 2–3 minutes. Toss the meat and return the lid, making sure the meat is brown and the flour isn't sticking, and cook for a couple more minutes. Remove the lid and add the wine, stirring to scrape up the bits off the bottom of the pan and make a thick gravy. Add the red currant jelly, and when it's dissolved add the stock. Establish a gentle simmer, then return the onion mixture to the pan and let cook very gently for about 15 minutes.

Meanwhile, trim and peel the carrots and slice thinly on the diagonal. Add the carrots to the stew and simmer for 5 minutes, then add the peas. Cook for a couple more minutes until the peas are tender, then check the seasoning and serve sprinkled with parsley.

Catalan veal stew with prunes

Serves 4–6   *30 minutes preparation: 90 minutes cooking*

I don't know about you, but it's not often that I buy red meat on an impulse with no special dish in mind. On one occasion, when there was a particularly long queue at my butcher, I had plenty of time to check out what was on offer. A fine display of various cuts of rosy-pink British veal caught my eye and, as I had vague thoughts of making a stew, I decided on stewing veal. By chance I came across this bizarre-sounding recipe in a book that I trust implicitly. Patience Gray's Honey From A Week, Fasting and Feasting in Tuscany, Catalonia, The Cyclades and Apulia *is so much more than a cook book. I feel sure everything has been cooked many times and this* estofada, *as they call stews in Catalonia, is exceptional. The prunes, incidentally, are cooked separately and served at one end of a large dish with a mound of fried potatoes at the other. Another odd-seeming ingredient is dark chocolate. Its effect is to thicken the sauce and give it a rich, glossy texture. It's a technique that pops up in some Italian stews and Mexican* mole *and its flavor is virtually imperceptible. I've taken the liberty of slightly adapting the recipe using canned tomatoes and ready-cooked prunes.*

2lb/1kg lean veal	½ tsp paprika
about 4 tbsp olive oil	pinch ground cinnamon
1 large onion	2 sprigs thyme
3 garlic cloves	1 bay leaf
4 canned peeled tomatoes	few sprigs parsley
1¼ cups dry white wine	12 large, soft dried prunes
2 tbsp Spanish brandy or whisky	fried potatoes to serve
2 squares semisweet chocolate	salt and freshly ground black pepper

Cut the veal into large kabob-size chunks. Heat some of the oil in a spacious, heavy-bottom flameproof casserole and brown the meat in uncrowded batches. Transfer to a plate as you finish.

Peel and slice the onion and brown it in the pan, with the peeled garlic cloves. Crush the tomatoes into the softened onion, then add the wine and brandy. Cook gently for about 15 minutes, or until the liquid has reduced by about half. Stir in the chocolate together with the paprika and cinnamon. Tie the thyme, bay leaf, and parsley in a bundle and add to the pan. Add the meat and its juices and sufficient water just to cover the meat.

Season with salt and pepper and simmer, covered, very gently for 1 hour. Check a piece of meat to see if it is tender; if not, cook for an additional 30 minutes. Simmer the prunes in a little water during the last 15 minutes of cooking. Serve the stew with the prunes and fried potatoes.

Parmesan veal scallops with arugula salad

Serves 2   *15 minutes preparation: 30 minutes cooking*

The smart way of making scallops is to do the whole job—the bashing and then the flouring—in waxed paper. This eliminates all the mess. The addition of grated Parmesan to the bread crumbs gives the scallops extra flavor, making them that bit more satisfying. I have stipulated veal for this simple but excellent, quick supper, but if you prefer, it would also work brilliantly with turkey or chicken. You can buy turkey scallops, but you will have to split a chicken breast fillet, opening it out like a book before proceeding. The idea is to end up with a super-thin piece of meat that has been teased into being double its size rather than battered and torn by too aggressive bashing. The salad is served, restaurant-style, on top of the meat, almost obscuring the scallop. It is one of those quick but stylish suppers that is perfect for any occasion and is sure to become a favorite. If you want to make the dish for more than two, increase the ingredients in proportion and keep the scallops warm in a low oven as you finish cooking each one.

2oz/55g bread without crusts	generous knob butter
¼ cup freshly grated Parmesan cheese, grated	3½oz/100g cherry tomatoes
1 egg	2oz/55g arugula
2 veal scallops	1 tbsp balsamic vinegar
flour for dusting	1 lemon (for wedges)
4 tbsp olive oil	salt and freshly ground black pepper

Blitz the bread to make fine crumbs. Transfer to a large plate or shallow bowl and mix the grated Parmesan into the crumbs. Whisk the egg in a second shallow bowl. Measure off a large double fold of waxed paper. Lay one scallop in the middle of one half and fold the other half over the top. Use a rolling pin to bash the scallop gently but firmly until it is the thickness of a coin and more than double its original size.

Dust both sides with flour, shaking away any excess, and repeat the process with the second scallop. Dip the scallops first in the egg and then in the bread crumbs and let rest while you heat 1 tablespoon of the olive oil and half the butter in a skillet. When it's hot, lay out one scallop in the skillet and cook, adjusting the heat so nothing burns, for about 2 minutes a side, or until the egg has set, the crumbs turned golden, and the meat is cooked through. Transfer to a warmed plate and repeat the process with the second scallop.

Quickly cut the tomatoes into fourths. Pile the arugula over the scallops, then scatter over the tomatoes and splash with the balsamic vinegar and remaining olive oil. Season with salt and pepper and serve with lemon wedges.

Corned beef hash with cilantro

Serves 2　*15 minutes preparation: 30 minutes cooking*

One unfortunate afternoon, the wife of the owner of my local small store in west London was alone behind the counter when half a dozen unfamiliar youths came into the premises. Within minutes, they had taken up strategic positions and she was powerless to stop a couple of them going upstairs to pilfer from her home. Fortunately there was no physical damage, but the shock was so great that the store has closed. It was a useful place for basic stuff such as potatoes, onions, corned beef, and tomatoes, which are necessary for this comforting childhood fry-up. I got the idea of jazzing up the hash with Indian seasonings from my store and, despite the depressing legacy now attached to the dish, it's such a good twist on an old favorite, that I want to pass on the details. To add a healthy note, serve the hash with steamed spinach.

1lb/500g potatoes	½ tsp ground coriander
3 shallots	3½oz/100g corned beef
1 small chile	2 plum tomatoes
2in/5cm piece fresh gingerroot	1 tbsp chopped fresh cilantro
1 garlic clove	2 large eggs
3 tbsp vegetable oil	salt and freshly ground black pepper
½ tsp ground turmeric	

Boil the potatoes in plenty of salted for about 15 minutes, or until tender. Place the pan under the cold tap and let it run for a couple of minutes. Drain and peel the potatoes, then cut into dice about the size of sugar lumps.

Meanwhile, peel and finely chop the shallots. Trim and split the chiles, scraping away the seeds. Slice into skinny strips and then into tiny dice. Peel the ginger and grate or finely chop. Peel and finely chop the garlic. Heat 1 tablespoon of the oil in a large skillet and stir in the shallots, chile, and garlic. Cook for about 5 minutes over medium heat until the shallots are beginning to soften. Stir in the turmeric and ground coriander and cook for a few more seconds, then squash the shallots against the side of the pan. Add another tablespoon of oil, then turn up the heat and add the potatoes. Scoop the shallots up over the potatoes and cook for 5 minutes over brisk heat.

Chunk the corned beef or crumble it coarsely if using ready-cut slices. Core the tomatoes, then chop quite small. Add the corned beef, tomatoes, and half the cilantro to the pan. Season generously with salt and pepper. Stir and let cook for 5 minutes. Scoop up the bottom layer and cook for an additional 10 minutes. Divide the hash between two hot plates. Add the remaining oil to the pan and quickly cook the eggs. Place an egg on top of each plate of hash and sprinkle with the last of the cilantro.

Albondigas wrap with cherry tomatoes and lettuce hearts

Serves 4   *15 minutes preparation: 20 minutes cooking*

On my first night in Barcelona I played Russian roulette at Cerveceria Catalana, one of this city's best tapas bars. Picking from a plate of deep fried little chiles called padrane, *I munched my way through half a dozen before I was hit by the explosive buzz. Recovery was quick thanks to other delicious morsels such as wafers of pungent Serrano ham with roasted red bell pepper and tomato-rubbed toast piled high with slippery salt cod with a smear of sweet tomato paste. I would grow very fat if I lived near this wonderful place. It is easy, for example, to spear through a bowl of* albondigas, *the herby miniature meatballs so beloved of tapas bars. They go well with spaghetti and a quick tomato sauce made by broiling, then blitzing cherry tomatoes, but I like them piled into warm pita bread envelopes with cherry tomatoes and crunchy lettuce hearts.*

1lb/500g cherry tomatoes
4 tbsp olive oil
1 tbsp balsamic vinegar
2oz/55g white bread, without crusts
1 plump garlic clove
2 tbsp milk or 1 tbsp cream or strained plain yogurt
1 onion
1lb/500g ground beef
3 tbsp finely chopped flatleaf parsley

½ tsp fresh thyme
generous pinch nutmeg, preferably freshly grated
1 egg
2 tbsp all-purpose flour
4 tbsp dry sherry, preferably Oloroso
4 Boston lettuce hearts
4 pita breads
salt and freshly ground back pepper

Put the tomatoes, 2 tablespoons of the olive oil, and the balsamic vinegar in a skillet and cook, shaking the pan occasionally, for 10–15 minutes, or until the tomatoes are soft and squashy but keeping their shape. Tip into a bowl to cool. Place the bread and peeled garlic clove in the bowl of a food processor and blitz into fine crumbs. Stir in the milk.

Peel and halve the onion, then finely chop. Add it to the food processor bowl with the meat, 2 tablespoons of the parsley, the thyme, nutmeg, ½ teaspoon salt, and a generous grating of black pepper. Beat the egg and then blitz in a few short bursts, until thoroughly blended and combined. Rinse your hands in cold water, then pinch off small lumps and roll between your hands into cherry-tomato-size balls.

Dust the meatballs with flour. Heat the remaining oil in the (cleaned) skillet over medium heat and cook the meatballs in batches, turning so they brown all over and cook through. Allow for about 10 minutes per batch. Remove them from the pan, then pour in the sherry and let bubble up and reduce to a sticky syrup. Return the meatballs and roll in the juices. Sprinkle on the remaining parsley. Trim and cut the lettuce hearts into fourths, then shred lengthwise. Warm the pitas, then split down one side and fill with meatballs, tomatoes, and lettuce. Eat at once.

Italian venison stew with Marsala

Serves 4–6   *30 minutes preparation: 90 minutes cooking*

The Italians have a lovely way of livening up the look and taste of stewed dishes with finely chopped parsley, lemon zest, and garlic. They call this fiesty seasoning gremolata *or* gremolada *and it works a treat with this interestingly gamey venison stew. In Italy it would be served with buttery polenta rather than mashed potato. I like it with plenty of crusty bread such as ciabatta. As always with stews, flavors mature if the dish is left overnight and reheated the next day.*

3oz/85g chopped pancetta or rindless smoked
  lean bacon
2 onions
3 garlic cloves
1 large sprig rosemary
½ stick butter
3 tbsp olive oil
2lb/1kg venison stewing steak, cut into large pieces
scant ½ cup red wine vinegar
⅔ cup red wine

2 chicken stock cubes
1 bay leaf
½ tsp ground cloves
10 juniper berries
½ tsp ground allspice
3 tbsp flour
1 small glass Marsala
small bunch flatleaf parsley
1 large unwaxed lemon
salt and freshly ground black pepper

Finely chop the pancetta. Peel and halve the onions, then finely chop. Peel the garlic and chop 2 cloves finely. Strip the leaves from the sprig of rosemary and chop very finely.

Heat half the butter and the oil in a large, heavy-bottom pan and stir in the pancetta, onions, garlic, and rosemary. Cook, stirring often, for 10 minutes, or until the onions are browned and the pancetta crisp. Increase the heat and add the venison. Brown the meat very thoroughly all over, then season generously with salt and pepper. Now add the vinegar, letting it cook into the meat while loosening the sticky brown goo at the bottom of the pan. Add the wine and let it bubble up, then cook for several minutes until reduced to a syrup. Dissolve the stock cubes in 4 cups boiling water and add half of it to the pan. Add the bay leaf, cloves, juniper berries, and ground allspice. Return the liquid to a simmer, then cover the pan and cook for 1 hour.

Melt the remaining butter in a small pan and stir in the flour to make a smooth, thick paste. Gradually add the remaining stock, stirring as it comes up to a boil, to make a smooth, thick sauce. Simmer for a couple of minutes then add to the stew. Return the stew to a boil and add the Marsala, then reduce the heat to a simmer and cook for 20 minutes, or until the meat is quite tender. Taste and adjust the seasoning with salt and pepper.

Strip the parsley leaves from the stems. Use a zester or potato peeler to remove the lemon zest in paper-thin sheets. Finely chop the parsley and lemon zest and the remaining garlic clove. Now chop all three together. Serve the stew with a sprinkling of the *gremolata*.

Picadillo with coconut chile rice

Serves 4 *15 minutes cooking: 35 minutes cooking*

Cooking ground beef with raisins, green olives, capers, tomatoes, and sweet bell peppers might sound odd but just you try it. The result is an interesting flavor with nuggets of sweet and sour. In Chile they serve it with rice and call it picadillo, *in Mexico they top it with cornmeal (polenta) and call it* tamale *pie and in the West Indies they spread it on mashed breadfruit, then roll it up like a jelly roll and call it* breadfruit sandwich. *The exact proportion of sweet/sour ingredients is a matter of taste, but this is an occasion when more is better than less. Rum punch would go well with this.*

1 onion
1 red or green bell pepper or 3 celery stalks
2 tbsp vegetable or sunflower oil
4 large garlic cloves
zest of 1 lime
1 small red or green chile
1½ cups basmati rice
7fl oz/200 ml carton coconut cream or canned
  coconut milk
1lb/500g good-quality ground beef
⅔ cup green olives

14oz/400g strained tomatoes or liquidized canned
  peeled tomatoes
2 tbsp raisins, preferably Spanish, Italian, or
  Australian (bigger, juicier, and sweeter)
2 tbsp capers
1 glass white wine, about ⅔ cup
Angostura bitters (optional)
2 tbsp chopped flatleaf parsley or cilantro
avocado slices and lime wedges to serve
salt and freshly ground black pepper

Peel and finely chop the onion. Finely chop the bell pepper, discarding the stem, seeds, and white membrane. If using celery, dice or slice thinly. Cook the onion and chopped bell pepper or celery in the oil in a spacious skillet or similarly wide-based pan. Stir a couple of times and cook for about 6 minutes, or until the onion is beginning to color.

Meanwhile, peel and finely chop the garlic. Use a zester or potato peeler to remove the lime zest in paper-thin sheets. Trim and split the chile and scrape away the seeds, then chop finely. Place the rice in a pan with the coconut milk, lime zest, and chile. Add scant ½ cup water. Bring to a boil, then turn down the heat to very low and cook, tightly covered, for 15 minutes. Leave, without removing the lid, for at least 5 minutes.

Add the meat to the onion, then increase the heat and cook, breaking up the lumps, for about 5 minutes. Add the next 5 ingredients plus a generous seasoning of salt and pepper. Stir well. Turn down the heat and simmer for 25–30 minutes, or until the sauce is thick but still wet. Taste and adjust the seasoning with salt, pepper, a squeeze of lime juice, and Angostura bitters if you have some.

Remove the lime zest from the rice. Serve the rice and picadillo together, garnished with the parsley, giving each serving 2 or 3 slices of avocado and a wedge of lime.

Indian venison burgers with cucumber raita

Serves 2   *15 minutes preparation: 20 minutes cooking*

Ground venison is a lean healthy option that is immensely versatile. Turn it into meatballs, for example, served, perhaps, in a plum, gin, and juniper sauce, as they do with the haunch of deer at Rules, an old-fashioned British restaurant in London's Covent Garden. Indian restaurants are very keen on venison and that is where the inspiration came from for these exceptionally delicious little burgers. I serve them with naan bread, which puffs and swells like pita bread in a hot oven and is the perfect envelope to hold the burgers. A good accompaniment is homemade raita, which is turned into a full-scale salad by adding plenty of big chunks of cucumber.

3½oz/100g shallots or red onion	1 tomato
2 tbsp vegetable oil	½ cucumber
1 small green chile	1 garlic clove
1 tsp ground cumin	1¼ cups plain yogurt
1 tsp ground coriander	1 tbsp olive oil
½ tsp ground turmeric	squeeze lemon juice
4 tbsp chopped cilantro	2 peshwari naan
2 venison grill steaks or 13oz/375g ground venison	salt

Peel and halve the shallots or onion, then finely chop. In a skillet, gently cook the shallots or onion in 1 tablespoon of the oil for several minutes, or until softened without much coloring. Meanwhile, split the chile and scrape away the seeds, then slice into skinny batons and across into tiny scraps. Add the chile, cumin, coriander, and turmeric to the pan, then stir and cook for about a minute before tipping the mixture into a mixing bowl.

Add 2 tablespoons of the chopped cilantro and the venison to the bowl and use your hands to mix and mulch thoroughly. Divide the mixture into four and form into even-size patties. Wipe out the skillet, then add the remaining oil and, when hot, cook the burgers over medium heat for 5 minutes a side, then reduce the heat and cook for an additional 3 minutes a side or until cooked through.

Meanwhile, make the raita. Dice the tomato. Split the cucumber and use a teaspoon to remove the seeds. Chop into small chunks. Peel and chop the garlic and crush to a paste with a little salt. Mix the garlic, olive oil and lemon juice into the yogurt, then add the tomato, cucumber chunks, and the remaining chopped cilantro. If convenient, preheat the oven to 400°F/200°C and heat up the naan. When they are puffed, halve the naan and serve the burgers and raita in the bread. Alternatively, warm the bread on a grill pan.

New York steak salad with horseradish

Serves 2   *15 minutes preparation: 10–15 minutes cooking*

This salad takes a leaf out of the Thai salad book. Theirs are packed with interesting textures and flavors and are usually a mix of hot and cold, cooked and raw, spicy and sweet flavors. There is none of the characteristic chile heat in this salad, but the crunch of tiny scraps of red onion mingling with lightly cooked string beans—the sort which have been sliced long and thin and end up looking like green spaghetti—wakens up the taste buds. Cherry tomatoes add a sweetness that lifts the flavors and provides a counterbalance to the creamy, horseradish-spiked salad dressing. This interesting mix of flavors goes well with steak, and when the steak is served Thai-salad-style in thinly sliced strips, it brings a touch of fashionable fusion presentation to a relatively straightforward dish.

13oz/375g thick sirloin steak	1 tbsp mayonnaise
2 tbsp olive oil	½ tbsp red wine vinegar
10oz/300g string beans, long cut	½ tbsp creamed horseradish
3½oz/100g cherry tomatoes	1 tbsp chopped flatleaf parsley
1 small red onion	salt and freshly ground black pepper

Smear the steak on both sides with slightly less than half the olive oil. Heat a ridged grill pan (or skillet) for several minutes until very hot. Season one side of the steak with salt and pepper and lay it, seasoned side down, in the pan. Use tongs or a spatula to press the steak down for maximum initial contact and cook for a couple of minutes until you see the contact meat turning brown and crusty. Season the uncooked surface, then turn and repeat. Depending on the thickness of the steak, this timing will produce a rare steak. If you like it cooked medium, turn the steaks again, cooking for an additional minute on each side. Lift the steak onto a cutting board and let stand for several minutes to relax.

Meanwhile, make the salad. Drop the beans into a large pan of salted boiling water and boil for 3 minutes. Drain carefully in a colander, shaking it several times. Halve the tomatoes through their middles, or lengthwise if plum cherry tomatoes. Peel and halve the onion, then finely chop. Spoon the mayonnaise into a mixing bowl and stir in the vinegar and creamed horseradish, then gradually beat in the remaining olive oil. Stir the chopped onion into the dressing. Add the beans, tomatoes, and parsley. Season lightly with salt and generously with black pepper and toss thoroughly.

Divide the salad between two plates. Trim any fat from the steak, then slice thinly across the width, cutting slightly at a slant. Drape the steak over the salad and drizzle the juices over the top. Eat now or later.

Smoked chili con carne with cherry tomatoes

Serves 4 *30 minutes preparation: 60 minutes cooking*

One of my favorite ingredients is "soft" La Chinata smoked paprika from the Extremadura region of Spain. Locally grown capsicums are dried over oak-wood fires to make a brick-red powder giving the otherwise mild and gentle paprika a distinctive smoky taste. I've used it in all sorts of dishes, but when combined with chili powder, cumin, and oregano, it gives this version of chili con carne a rich and robust flavor that completely alters the dish. Another surprise addition is cherry tomatoes. These are added at the end of cooking and cook to a seductive melting consistency which injects a fresh, sweet acidity into most mouthfuls. The chili heat is perfect for me; if you want to blow your head off rather than enjoy the subtlety of the dish, tune it up with Tabasco. Serve it over a mound of steaming rice.

4 rindless strips smoked lean bacon
3 tbsp vegetable oil
2 onions
2 large garlic cloves
1 small unwaxed lemon
1lb 10oz/750g lean beef
2 heaped tsp smoked paprika
1 heaped tsp each chili powder, ground cumin,
  and dried oregano
½ tbsp all-purpose flour

2 glasses red wine
7oz/200g canned chopped tomatoes
1 chicken stock cube dissolved in generous 2 cups
  hot water
1 bay leaf
9oz/250g cherry tomatoes
14oz/400g canned red kidney beans
⅔ cup sour cream
small bunch chives
salt

Cut the bacon across the strips into strips. Heat 1 tablespoon of the oil in a skillet. Cook, gently at first, until crisp. Scoop it out onto a large plate. Meanwhile, peel and chop the onions and garlic. Cook both in the bacon oil, adding a big pinch of salt, for about 6 minutes, or until slippery and lightly browned. Remove the zest from half the lemon and shred or cut into scraps. Stir zest into the onion; cook for two minutes. Tip the onion mixture into the bacon.

Chop the beef into pieces about half the size of kabob chunks. Using the rest of the oil, brown the meat in batches in the skillet, so it gets crusty rather than juicy, transferring the batches to a plate as you go. Return all the meat to the pan. Sprinkle the paprika, chili, cumin, oregano, and 1 teaspoon salt over the meat, then stir well and cook for a couple of minutes before stirring in the flour. Cook for a minute or so.

Add the wine, then stir well and cook over medium heat for 5–10 minutes, or until reduced by half. Add the canned tomatoes, stock, and bay leaf. Simmer, uncovered, over medium heat for 30 minutes, or until the meat is tender and the liquid reduced. Taste and adjust the seasoning with salt and lemon juice. Add the cherry tomatoes and simmer for 5 minutes. Tip the beans into a strainer, then rinse with cold water and shake dry. Add the beans to the pan. Cook for an additional 5 minutes. Serve with a dollop of sour cream and garnish of snipped chives.

Spag bol Florentine

Serves 4–6   *15 minutes preparation: 60 minutes cooking*

Thick, terra-cotta brown, and rich with flavor. The Florentine bit refers to spinach. This gives the sauce a splash of color and you your greens. Leave it out if you like. Ragu *improves if it is left overnight. Serve with spaghetti or your favorite pasta. It is also good rolled up in blanched cabbage leaves with a chunky tomato sauce, in wraps, and for making "instant" lasagna with soak-and-go lasagna squares.*

4 rindless strips lean bacon
½ stick butter
1 tbsp cooking oil
1 onion
2 carrots
2 celery stalks
1lb/450g ground beef
1 large glass red wine or ½ chicken stock cube dissolved in 1 cup hot water
⅔ cup milk
¼ tsp grated nutmeg, 2–3 gratings if using whole nutmeg
1 cup strained tomatoes (or 14oz/400g canned whole tomatoes, puréed and strained)
squeeze lemon juice
generous 1 cup young leaf spinach
salt and freshly ground black pepper

Dice the bacon. Heat half the butter and the oil in a heavy-bottom pan over medium heat and cook the bacon until crisp. Remove from the pan. Meanwhile, peel and finely chop the onion and the carrots. Trim and peel the celery and finely chop (including the leaves, if there are any). Add the onion to the pan and cook for a couple of minutes before adding the carrots and celery. Cook for 5 minutes, stirring a couple of times, then add the meat.

Stir as it changes from pink to brown. Season generously with salt. Add the wine and increase the heat to medium-high. Cook, stirring occasionally, until all the wine has evaporated. Add the milk and nutmeg. Continue to cook, stirring frequently, and when the milk has almost entirely disappeared (it takes about 10 minutes) add the strained tomatoes. Return the bacon to the pan. Cook at a gentle simmer, uncovered, for 45 minutes.

Taste the *ragu*, adjusting the seasoning with salt, pepper, and a squeeze of lemon juice. Cook uncovered for at least 15 minutes, or until thick and moist rather than wet. Stir the spinach into the *ragu* and cook for about 5 minutes, or until wilted and integrated into the sauce. Stir in the remaining butter and serve.

Thai beef salad with grapes

Serves 4   *20 minutes preparation: 10 minutes cooking*

Thai salads are perfect if you're trying to shed pounds because they contain hardly any oil. Instead, the dressing is sweet and sour, pungent, and as chile hot as you like. Any Thai beef salad I've ever eaten has been made with quickly seared beef that is crusty on the outside but pink within. Don't bother with this salad unless you chose a decent piece of steak, because it must be very tender. It's the crunchy vegetables that should exercise your jaws. The sweetness from the grapes is a lovely fresh surprise. There is plenty here for four big eaters, but a bowl of hot new potatoes tossed with mint would be a lovely accompaniment.

scant 1½ cups green beans
1 large garlic clove
1–2 small red chiles
2 tbsp Thai fish sauce (*nam pla*)
½ tbsp brown sugar
½ tbsp soy sauce or oyster sauce
2 limes
2 red onions

½ cucumber
1 celery heart
½oz/15g bunch cilantro
3½oz/100g seedless red grapes
1 large rump steak, about 13oz/375g
1 tbsp cooking oil
½oz/15g bunch mint
salt and freshly ground black pepper

Put a large pan of salted water on to boil. Trim the beans and cut them in half. Add the beans to the boiling water. Cook for 2 minutes, then drain and splash with cold water to cool. Peel and finely chop the garlic. Sprinkle with a little salt and work to a paste. Split the chile or chiles and scrape away the seeds, then slice into skinny batons and chop into tiny dice. Place the garlic and chile in a salad bowl. Add the fish sauce, brown sugar, soy sauce, and juice of the limes. Stir well. Peel and halve the onions, then finely slice, cutting down rather than across the halves. Stir the onions into the dressing; after a few minutes they will wilt slightly.

Peel the cucumber and split it lengthwise, then scrape out the seeds and their watery surround. Slice the cucumber into half moons. Trim the celery heart and peel the outer stems if they look stringy. Slice across the heart as finely as you can. Tip into a colander and rinse under cold running water. Shake dry. Place the cucumber and celery on top of the onions. Coarsely chop the cilantro leaves and halve the grapes. Add both to the salad.

To cook the steak, heat a grill pan (or skillet) until very hot. Rub the steak with cooking oil and season one side with salt and pepper. Slap the seasoned side down onto the grill pan and press it down hard with a spatula, holding it there for 1 minute. Season the exposed side with salt and pepper, then turn the steak and repeat. Depending on the thickness of the steak and how rare you like it, either remove the steak to rest or repeat the cooking on each side. Let the steak sit for 5 minutes before you season it again and slice it very thinly. Toss the salad. Add the steak and any juices and toss again. Coarsely chop the mint and scatter over the top. Eat.

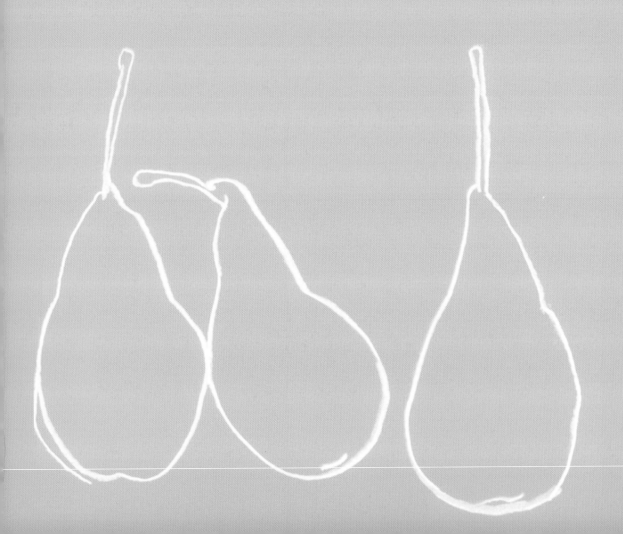

Desserts

One of my best friends is what I'd call a dessertaholic. In my restaurant-reviewing days, we once went to Langan's Brasserie in London and had a four-course meal entirely of desserts. We started with raspberries and vanilla ice cream, followed with rice pudding (with strawberry jelly), went on to treacle tart, and finished with something very dark and intensely chocolaty. Throughout our "meal" we drank champagne. I can't say I'd rush to repeat the experience, but I do like to finish a meal with something sweet. At home, I'm usually on the look-out for something quick and easy to make and I either want a fresh and light dessert or a gorgeous bowl of stodge to sink my spoon into. I am particularly fond of rice puddings and include here four very different ones, all of which can be cooked over direct heat. This sort of filling pudding suits the times when my sweet tooth kicks in and it becomes the main part of the meal. As before, all these recipes are cooked or prepared in one pan and are served in a bowl rather than on a plate.

Moroccan rice pudding

Serves 6   *15 minutes preparation: 30 minutes cooking*

When rice pudding is mentioned, anyone brought up in Britain will know what you're talking about. It either comes out of a can and is very sweet and creamy, or it has been baked in the oven until the milk forms a floppy brown skin. Both are bland and traditionally served in large portions. There are those among us who love both types, especially when it is eaten with a dusting of caster sugar, a dollop of thick cream, and a scoop of strawberry jelly. Moroccan rice pudding is quite different.

In Morocco, the milk they use is often flavored with ground almonds and the pudding is cooked with cinnamon and only a hint of sugar. They use round-grain "pudding" rice, but it is cooked slowly in a pan until the rice swells with absorbed milk and clings together in a loose creamy sauce. A knob of butter or, in my adaptation, a scoop of cream, combines with a slug of orange-flower water to point up the flavors. The perfect contrast is a garnish of toasted almonds and pistachios.

⅓ cup ground almonds
2½ cups milk
1 cinnamon stick
2in/5cm strip orange zest
1 vanilla bean
generous ¾ cup pudding rice
2oz/55g unrefined organic cane sugar
3 tbsp orange-flower water
4 tbsp heavy cream

small knob butter
2 tbsp shredded almonds
handful skinned pistachios
cinnamon for dusting
sliced oranges dusted with confectioners' sugar
    and cinnamon, and thick cream or strained plain
    yogurt to serve (optional)
salt

Place the ground almonds in a medium-sized pan with 1 cup boiling water. Boil for 2 minutes, then add the milk, cinnamon stick, orange zest, vanilla bean, and a pinch of salt. Bring to boiling point while stirring constantly, tthen turn down the heat and simmer for 5 minutes.

Add the rice to the pan. Simmer very gently, stirring occasionally, for about 20 minutes, or until the rice is tender and most of the liquid absorbed. Stir in the sugar. Add the orange-flower water and 2 tablespoons of the heavy cream and cook for 1 more minute, or until thick but sloppy. Let cool in the pan. When tepid, remove the cinnamon stick and vanilla bean (both can be wiped and re-used) and break up the orange zest into little scraps. Stir in the rest of the cream.

Transfer to a serving bowl. Melt the knob of butter in a skillet, then add the shredded almonds and toss until golden. Drain on absorbent paper towels and use to garnish the rice pudding. Coarsely chop the pistachios and add them too. Dust with cinnamon and, if liked, serve with sliced oranges dusted with confectioners' sugar and cinnamon, and thick cream.

Cranachan

Serves 6   *10 minutes preparation: 5 minutes cooking*

A plate of perfect raspberries lightly dusted with superfine sugar and served with homemade vanilla ice cream is, for me, a Desert Island dessert. The finest raspberries come from Scotland and the Scots have a delicious tradition of combining them with whisky-whipped cream and toasted oatmeal. I give here the basic recipe for Cranachan, but it is one of those dishes that is open to interpretation: more whisky, more sugar, more raspberries, or more crunchy oats. Whatever. Suit yourself. Get in the swing of things by serving it with shortbread cookies and a wee dram.

2oz/55g jumbo or ordinary porridge oats
1¼ cups whipping cream
2 tbsp runny honey or confectioners' sugar

3 tbsp whisky
2⅔ cups ripe raspberries

Sprinkle the oats over a wide, heavy-bottom pan such as a roasting pan or large skillet and place over moderate heat, shaking occasionally, until toasted and golden. Remove from the pan to cool.

Pour the cream into a mixing bowl and whip with the honey until it begins to form peaks. Fold in the whisky, then three-quarters of the raspberries and three-quarters of the toasted oats.

Divide the mixture between six glass bowls or transfer to a suitable serving bowl. Garnish with the remaining raspberries and oats. Dust with a little more confectioners' sugar or with a drizzle of whisky. Chill and serve.

Eton mess

Serves 6   *20 minutes preparation*

Eton mess is a strawberry fool with a name that links it to one of England's most famous public schools. Occasionally it pops up on restaurant menus, in magazines, and cook books, and the common denominator is strawberries and cream, although no two recipes are the same. At Eton, apparently, a "mess" means taking tea in your room with "a mess" of one or two other boys. One friend remembered a banana mess of mashed banana with two scoops of ice cream and loads of cream, and thought the strawberry version something that might be served at the picnic held every year on June 4 to celebrate the birthday of King George III. It is not surprising that the half dozen or so Old Etonians I consulted had never eaten Eton mess, because the College chef confirmed that it hasn't been on the menu for years. Fortunately, because it's a great dish, their librarian dug out the Eton College recipe, dated 1936, and mentioned the name Pellaprat, a famous French chef who is regarded with the same reverence as Escoffier. It seems likely that he invented the dish when a load of overripe strawberries needed eating up. His disguise was a fluff of whipped cream and the fool was served with ladyfingers. Somewhere along the line, someone else had the idea of stirring chunks of meringue into the fool at the last moment. If you make your own meringues or buy good-quality ones, they give it delicious bursts of sweet, light crunch with a slight chew.

1lb 10oz/750g very ripe English strawberries
2 tbsp superfine sugar

1¾ cups whipping cream
12 mini meringues

Quickly rinse the strawberries under cold running water and shake dry. Remove the stems—the neatest way to do this is with a small, sharp knife, cutting at an angle around and under the stem, to remove a small cone, turning the strawberry rather than the knife. Leave small strawberries whole, halve medium ones, and cut large fruit into fourths. Place the fruit in a bowl, then sprinkle over the sugar and let it melt and turn the strawberries juicy. Toss and let stand for at least 10 minutes.

Whip the cream in the bowl in which you intend serving the fool, until it is thick, fluffy, and holds soft peaks. Drain the juices from the strawberries into the cream. Give a quick stir and then add the strawberries. Stir, crushing some of the strawberries as you mix. Cut the meringues into fourths and loosely fold them into the cream.

If you prefer, hold back half the strawberries, then pass them through a strainer directly into the fool, stirring to get swirls of seed-free strawberry purée.

Green fruit salad with avocado cream

Serves 4   *20 minutes preparation*

Kiwifruit was first introduced into the UK in 1953 and remained something of a mystery until the seventies when it became a cliché of nouvelle cuisine—*or small food on big plates, as it was known. Slices of its green pulp with distinctive black seeds adorned everything from fruit salads and gateaux to fans of duck breast with raspberry* coulis. *When someone discovered the high vitamin C content of kiwifruit—ten times more than the equal weight of a lemon—it caught on in a minor way as a health food. It's useful, too, in the fruit bowl, because it keeps well and brings a bit of unexpected color to fruit salads. Baby kiwi are about the same size as a large cherry tomato and their shiny, smooth skin is dark green. Unlike normal kiwi, which often need a few days in a warm kitchen before they are ready to eat, baby kiwi are sold ripe and ready to eat. They will appeal to anyone who likes sweet fruit and for my taste they work best in a salad with plenty of acidity to counterbalance their sweetness. I came across avocado cream in Spain, but think the idea probably originated in Brazil. It's a lovely dessert in its own right, but goes very well with this green fruit salad.*

4oz/125g kiwifruit (use baby ones if you can
    find them)
7oz/200g white grapes
4 ripe Conference pears
5 tbsp lime juice

2 oranges
4 passion fruit
2 ripe avocados
4 tbsp superfine sugar

Peel the baby kiwi, then slice them in two or three circles and transfer to a mixing bowl. Halve the grapes lengthwise or cut into fourths depending on their size. Remove the stems from the pears and cut them into fourths lengthwise. Cut out the core and cut into dice about the size of a sugar lump. Scoop the grapes and pear into the bowl and add 1 tablespoon of lime juice. Halve the oranges and squeeze the juice over the fruit salad. Toss everything together. Halve the passion fruit and scrape the contents of the shell over the top.

Run a sharp knife round the avocados and twist apart. Discard the pit and use a spoon to scrape the flesh into a small bowl. Add the remaining lime juice and the sugar and use a fork to mash and mix everything together, stirring to make a smooth, thick, green cream. Taste and adjust the seasoning with extra lime juice or sugar.

Place a scoop of the avocado cream in the middle of four serving dishes. Spoon over the fruit salad, making sure each serving has a decent share of passion fruit.

Chocolate and almond rice pudding

Serves 6–8   *15 minutes preparation: 30 minutes cooking*

Here's a lovely recipe for rice pudding that turns it into something unexpectedly special. I've always found it curious how little rice is needed to make rice pudding. My mother cooked hers for hours and hours in a very low oven and it always emerged with a thick, dark brown skin which flopped like a wet mackintosh the minute her serving spoon sought out the creamy rice within. We ate it with homemade jelly, sugar, and pouring cream and everyone except my oldest brother loved it dearly. I'm a big fan of the other way of cooking rice pudding in quasi-risotto style in a pan over direct heat. This method speeds up the cooking, although you will notice that as the rice cools it will thicken even more. I've taken a tip from the Aztecs (who discovered chocolate) and added a dried red chile to the milk. Don't be alarmed. It gives the finished dish the weeniest hint of chile, which combines with orange zest and cardamom to lift the flavors without dominating them. The crowning glory of this mysterious dark brown rice pudding is a generous drizzle of melted chocolate. If you serve the pudding warm, it gives puddles of intense flavor, but if you let it cool right down the chocolate sets hard. Serve as it is or with sour cream or strained plain yogurt.

generous ¾ cup pudding rice
1 small dried red chile
2 x 2in/5cm strips orange zest
3 cardamom pods
3½ cups milk
⅓ cup hot chocolate powder

2 heaped tsp cocoa powder
½ stick butter
½ cup slivered almonds
2 squares 70 percent dark chocolate
salt

Place the rice, chile, orange zest, cardamom seeds, and milk in a heavy-bottom pan over low heat. Add a pinch of salt and stir for a few minutes to stop the rice from sticking while the milk heats up. Simmer very gently, stirring occasionally, for about 20 minutes, or until the rice is tender and most of the liquid absorbed.

Remove and discard the chile, orange zest, and cardamom seeds. Stir in the hot chocolate powder, cocoa powder, and most of the butter. Melt the remaining butter in a skillet, then add the slivered almonds and toss until golden. Drain on absorbent paper towels and chop coarsely.

Stir most of the almonds into the pudding and transfer to a serving bowl. Garnish the top with the remaining almonds. Break the chocolate into chunks and place in a small bowl. Suspend the bowl over simmering water and stir until melted. Zigzag the melted chocolate over the top of the pudding. Serve lukewarm or cold.

Apple cream with banana passion fruit sauce

Serves 4–6   *15 minutes preparation: 15 minutes cooking*

I have a love-hate relationship with bananas. I only really like them when they're just ripe and there's a slight resistance as you bite. What I can't bear is when the flesh starts going woolly with a pear-drop whiff that tends to repeat. And repeat. One Saturday I happened to wander past my local fruit and veg market when my regular stall was flogging off dirt-cheap bananas. For £1 I came away with enough bananas to relive all my childhood favorites. I'd forgotten how much I love banana sandwiches, especially when they're made with super-fresh white bread and a generous sprinkling of superfine sugar. And mashed banana with sugar and milk, and banana custard, banana milk shake, and banana fritters.

Banana overkill led to the invention of this sauce, and although I've teamed it with fluffy apple purée and vanilla ice cream, it would go well with either on their own and would be a different thing to try with crêpes. It could be used in place of custard, but is good, too, with custard. As for the ice cream—well, you buy that.

For the sauce:
2 ripe but firm bananas
juice ½ lemon
2 tbsp runny honey
2 tbsp superfine sugar
scant ½ cup cold water
3 passion fruit

For the apple cream:
2 cooking apples
squeeze of lemon juice
¼ stick butter
2–4 tbsp raw brown sugar
good-quality vanilla ice cream—to serve

To make the sauce, peel the bananas and cut into circles. Place in a pan with the lemon juice, honey, sugar, and scant ½ cup water and boil for 5 minutes. Transfer to a blender and blitz for about 1 minute, or until smooth and fluffy. Pour into a bowl and let cool.

Cut the apples into fourths. Peel and core, then chop coarsely, working as quickly as you can before they discolor. Place in the pan with the lemon juice and generous ¾ cup water, then cover the pan and boil hard until the apples have collapsed—about 6 minutes. Use a potato masher to finish off puréeing the apples, then stir in the butter and 2 tablespoons of the sugar. Stir until the sugar dissolves. Taste, adding extra sugar if required. Transfer to a serving bowl, passing it through a strainer for a super-smooth finish. Let it cool off.

When the banana sauce is cold, cut the passion fruit in half round their middles. Use a teaspoon to gouge out the seeds and juices directly into the sauce. To serve, place two big scoops of ice cream in a bowl, then spoon over a generous dollop of warm apple purée and top with the chilled banana and passion fruit sauce. If you prefer, keep the passion fruit separate and add as a garnish.

Poached pears with lemon and lavender

Serves 6   *15 minutes preparation: 30 minutes cooking*

People used to make a special detour to see the lavender bush that flourished outside my mother's house on Chislehurst Common in Kent. Each year it grew bigger and more spectacular, echoing the stupendous bushes, nay fields of bushes, of purple lavender that grow around Grasse in the south of France. As far as I can recall, it was never used for cooking, although its aromatic fragrance always reminded me of rosemary and still makes me think of roast lamb. Although I've not seen lavender on sale in a food store, it is easy enough to come by from gardens. Flower heads lend a subtle and haunting elegance to all sorts of dishes and work wonderfully well in pears poached in white wine sweetened with honey and lifted by lemon zest. Poached pears are always a lovely dessert at any time of the year. I like them cold, served standing in the reduced juices of their poaching liquid, and would suggest accompanying them with sour cream or good-quality vanilla ice cream that is softened slightly more than is usual. Pinot gris, incidentally, is the grape variety used in Alsace wines. Any white wine would work in this recipe, although I would avoid anything very sweet.

6 lavender stems
about 2½ cups Alsace white wine
2 scant tbsp runny honey or sugar

1 unwaxed lemon
6 even-size Conference pears
6 tbsp sour cream

Place the lavender flowerheads in a pan that can hold the pears comfortably in a single layer. Add the wine and honey or sugar. Remove 2 paper-thin strips of zest from the lemon. Add them to the pan. Place the pan over medium-low heat and gently bring to a boil, swirling the pan a few times until the sugar dissolves or the honey melts. Boil the liquid hard for a couple of minutes to burn off the alcohol.

Meanwhile, carefully peel the pears, removing all the skin but leaving the stem intact. Use a small, sharp knife to remove the core in a small cone shape. Place the pears in the pan and reduce the heat, then cover the pan and cook for about 20 minutes, turning the pears once half way through cooking, until cooked through. Remove the pears to a serving dish, standing them up, and let cool.

Remove the lavender and lemon zest from the pan and cook the liquid at a steady simmer until reduced to a quarter of the original quantity. It will be slightly syrupy. Pour the liquid over the pears, so they glisten. Serve immediately with the sour cream, or wait until the liquid is cold.

Plum and amaretti instant trifle

Serves 4   *15 minutes preparation: 10 minutes cooking*

*I'm thrilled with this recipe. It is so simple to make and so delicious, with the added advantage
that it could be adapted for as few or as many people as required. The first time I made it,
I used the remains of a bottle of sweet and fizzy muscadet grape white wine to cook the plums.
The next time I improvised with a glass of white wine, a little honey, and sugar, but, if the
plums are really ripe, you shouldn't need extra sugar, and water would do just as well as wine.
Soft almond macroons are sold in a powder-blue box of 9oz/250g and are really worth searching
out for their dense but light texture and intense almond flavor. A firm sponge cake, such as an
all-butter lemon pound cake, is an acceptable alternative. If you are making this for a dinner
party, have everything ready and assemble the trifle at the last moment, either in individual
bowls or one big one. And if you want to be a bit flash, drizzle Amaretti liqueur over the
macaroons. The ice cream isn't essential to the success of the pudding.*

1lb/500g ripe plums (damsons, unless pitted after
 cooking, aren't suitable)
about ⅔ cup white wine or water
2 tbsp sugar
1 tbsp flavorless cooking oil

½ cup slivered almonds
5oz/150g soft almond macaroons (*amaretti morbidi*)
 or all-butter lemon pound cake
4 scoops of vanilla ice cream (optional)
¾–1¼ cups strained plain yogurt

Cut the plums off their pits in big chunks. Put them in a pan with the wine and sugar.
Cover the pan and simmer vigorously for 5–6 minutes, or until the pieces of plum are tender.
Tip into a dish and let chill or pop into the freezer for about 10 minutes.

Meanwhile, heat the oil in a skillet placed over medium heat and when hot add the almonds.
Toss constantly until lightly golden. Tip onto paper towels to drain.

Cut the macaroons into fourths or cut the cake into 1in/2.5cm chunks. Place in four dishes,
then spoon over some of the plum juices to saturate partially. Top with a scoop of ice cream,
if using, then cover with yogurt. Spoon over some of the plums and top with more yogurt, then
sprinkle with the toasted almonds. Serve immediately. Yum.

Orange and vanilla poached apricots

Serves 6   *10 minutes preparation: 30 minutes cooking*

I often find myself casting around at the last moment for something to serve for dessert. Fresh fruit salad is a favorite, but dried fruit is useful too. Dried fruit used to need lengthy soaking and cooking, but these days you can buy so-called no-soak dried fruit. A packet of these apricots, for example, is a great thing to keep in the pantry. I particularly like them poached in fresh orange juice and honey, and if I happen to have a vanilla bean, that goes in too. It flecks the juices with tiny black spots and enhances the flavors of this beguiling fruit. Poached like this, it could then be wrapped in puff pastry, perhaps with a slice of creamy goat cheese, and baked until flaky and golden. I tend to do nothing more than leave the apricots to cool and serve them over a generous scoop of thick, creamy organic yogurt. Another neat idea is to stuff each apricot with an almond. As the fruit cooks, the almonds soften and flavor the apricots from the inside. Don't forget to warn guests that the "pit" is edible.

9oz/250g no-soak apricots
scant ¼ cup blanched almonds
1 tbsp runny honey

2 large oranges
1 vanilla bean
plain yogurt to serve

Slip an almond inside each apricot in place of its absent pit. Place the fruit in a small pan with the honey. Use a sharp potato peeler to remove two 2in/5cm strips of wafer-thin orange zest from one of the oranges. Chop it very finely and add to the pan. Place a strainer over the pan to catch the seeds and squeeze over the juice from both oranges. It should just cover the apricots.

Tuck the vanilla bean down among the fruit. Place the pan over medium heat and bring slowly to a boil, stirring a few times to melt and disperse the honey. Reduce the heat to low, then partially cover the pan and simmer gently for 30 minutes. During this time the apricots will swell and absorb about half of the orange juice. Tip into a serving bowl and let cool.

Don't bother to remove the vanilla bean until the fruit is cold. Then it can be wiped and used again. Spoon the fruit over a mound of yogurt to serve.

Red fruit salad with raspberry cream

Serves 2–4   *20 minutes preparation: 5 minutes cooking*

Not so long ago there was only one sort of fruit salad. It came with chunks of unpeeled apple, grapes with seeds, and orange with pith and skin. With the tiniest bit of care and thought, it is easy to whip up fabulous fruit salads that are easy on the eye as well as being a good balance of texture and flavor. I like making a meal of fruit salad. Sometimes I eat nothing else. This version is a particular favorite. The inclusion of a few tart red currants and chunks of pink or red grapefruit provides just enough sharpness to make the other sweeter fruits taste better than ever. The quantities given would be about right for four as a dessert but are envisaged as the main part of supper for two. Griddle cakes are a delicious accompaniment.

1½ cups strawberries
scant 1 cup red currants
2 pink or red grapefuit
7oz/200g cherries
7oz/200g Flame or other seedless red grapes

2 oranges
1 cup strained plain yogurt
1 cup raspberries
confectioners' sugar
4–8 griddle cakes

Place all the fruit in a suitable bowl as you prepare it. Quickly rinse the strawberries before hulling them. If the strawberries are very big, cut them into chunks. Cut medium-size strawberries in half and leave small fruit whole. Rinse the red currants and pull them off the stems.

Cut the ends off the grapefruit to reveal the pink flesh and slice the remaining skin off the fruit in big pieces. Work round the grapefruit, cutting the flesh off the "core" in four or five pieces. Cut each piece into chunks. Cut the flesh off the cherry pits in four or five chunks. Cut the grapes into fourths or cut in two or three slices. Halve the oranges and squeeze their juice over the fruit. Toss. Spoon the yogurt into the middle of the salad.

Tip the raspberries into a strainer suspended over a bowl and sprinkle them with about ½ tablespoon confectioners' sugar. Using a spoon, press the raspberries through the strainer until only the seeds remain. Scrape under the strainer to collect all the pulp. Spoon the purée over the yogurt. Preheat the overhead broiler and lightly toast the pancakes. Dust them with confectioners' sugar and serve with the fruit salad.

Strawberry custard fool with balsamico

Serves 6   *20 minutes preparation*

*I happened on the idea of combining strawberries with balsamic vinegar by accident years ago,
little realizing it had been "invented" by., I think I'm right in saying, the Italian food writer
Anna del Conte. My inspiration came from Michel Guerard's recipe for fresh fruit steeped in
flavored and concentrated red wine. It's one of several wizard desserts which have inspired me
over the years from* Cuisine Minceur, *Guerard's seminal gourmet dieting book. Strawberries,
I discovered, work particularly well. So why not, I thought, try balsamic vinegar instead of
wine? It is, after all, the must from specially cultivated varieties of grape, which is fermented,
concentrated, and matured in Modena, to get that special spicy, rich, peppery yet creamy, and
tangy flavor. It might sound odd, but if you aren't familiar with the combination I do urge you
to give it a try. It is delicious alone or with strained plain yogurt. My latest variation on this
theme is this fool. It went down so well when I first made it that it has become a regular, which
is whipped up when a luscious quick dessert is the order of the day. It is blissfully easy to make,
and relies, as I often do, on ready-made fresh custard. It will keep without spoiling in the
refrigerator for 24 hours, but it is the sort of thing to make, then chill for an hour and eat.
If you do want to keep it waiting, add the toasted almonds just before you serve.*

1 lb/500g strawberries
2 tsp sugar
1 tbsp balsamic vinegar

generous 1 cup mascarpone
generous 1 cup ready-made fresh custard
2 tbsp toasted almonds

Rinse the strawberries and remove their stems. Set aside 6 strawberries. Cut the bulk of the
strawberries into fourths lengthwise, then put into a mixing bowl. Sprinkle with the sugar and
then add the balsamic vinegar. Toss with a spoon and let stand for 10 minutes, then toss
again and repeat if the sugar hasn't dissolved.

Meanwhile, crush the reserved whole strawberries through a strainer with the back of a
spoon into a bowl. Place the mascarpone in a serving bowl or second mixing bowl. Drain the
marinated strawberry juices into the mascarpone together with half the crushed strawberry
juice. Beat briefly until slackened and smooth. Tip the marinated strawberries and any
remaining juices into the mascarpone and amalgamate. Add the custard and loosely fold into
the mascarpone.

Swirl the remaining crushed strawberry juice over the top and loosely fold in to give color.
Cover with plastic wrap and chill for at least 1 hour. Scatter the almonds over the top.
If preferred, transfer to individual dishes before adding the strawberry juice and almonds.

White chocolate and raspberry trifle

Serves 6   *20 minutes preparation: 5 minutes cooking, plus cooling time*

As a child, I was never very keen on trifle, but as a so-called grown up I love having fun with it. I think it is very classy to simplify this childhood treat. I like to restrict the colors and flavors of the ingredients, so that the flavors and textures don't have to compete with each other. Dried apricots, for example, stewed in orange juice with vanilla, and with a decoration of silver balls and dark green gelatin leaves, looks as stunning as it tastes. This trifle is classy in the extreme. White chocolate and raspberries go together almost as well as peaches and cream. They are the perfect partners in trifle.

2 cups raspberries
juice ½ lime
1 tbsp Kirsch, vodka, or Framboise de Bourgogne
     liquer
2 tbsp confectioners' sugar

1 jelly roll (not chocolate)
4 squares white chocolate
⅔ cup heavy or whipping cream
2 x 18fl oz/500ml cartons fresh custard
few sprigs mint

Place ⅔ cup of raspberries in a strainer placed over a bowl. Use the back of a spoon to push all their juice through into the bowl, leaving the seeds behind. Scrape under the strainer so nothing is wasted. Add the lime juice and Kirsch, then sift 1 tablespoon of confectioners' sugar over the top. Stir well.

Slice the jelly roll about ½ in/1cm thick and use most of the slices to cover the base and make a single layer up the sides of a nice glass bowl. Moisten the slices with most of the raspberry juice and scatter with another ⅔ cup of raspberries. Set aside ¾ square of the chocolate and break the rest up into small pieces. Place the broken chocolate in a bowl and place the bowl inside another bowl filled with boiling water. Stir until the chocolate melts. This takes a few minutes, but if you want to speed it up, bring a small pan of water to a boil and suspend the bowl over the top. When it has melted, stir 1 tablespoon of the cream into the chocolate and then stir the mixture into 1 of the cartons of custard.

Pour half the chocolate custard over the prepared jelly roll and lay the remaining slices on top. Drizzle the remaining raspberry sauce over the slices and scatter with most of the remaining raspberries, reserving about 10 to decorate the top of the trifle. Use about half the second carton of custard to cover the trifle completely. Whip the rest of the cream until stiff and lift up scoops with a fork to decorate the top of the trifle.

Add the reserved raspberries. Grate the remaining chocolate on the large hole of a cheese grater over the top. Plant the mint sprigs here and there and dust the trifle with the rest of the confectioners' sugar. Cover with plastic wrap and chill for a minimum 2 hours and for up to 24 hours. Serve with the remaining custard.

Index

Acknowledgments

Many people contributed to the compilation of this book in one way or another but I particularly want to thank the staff at the 'golden triangle' of local food shops in my part of west London. They include my butcher Rodney Macken (and staff) of Macken and Bros., Dan Mortimer and staff at delicatessen, Mortimer & Bennett, Phil Diamond and his staff at Covent Garden Fishmonger, and Andrew Georghiou and staff at greengrocer C&M. Thanks too to Thai restaurant Sabai Sabai, supportive friends Andrew Payne, Helen Scott-Lidgett and Robert Osborne, my agent Bruce Hunter, son Zach John and his girlfriend Fiona Verdon-Smith for design ideas and other son Henry John, who ate most things in this book and drew the lovely illustrations. Thanks too to Joy Davies who made the food look so appetising for photography. I would particularly like to thank Bernice Davison, my original editor at the *Evening Standard*, and my mother, Jean Bareham, whose legacy paid for my lovely new kitchen, the building of which inspired this book.